BFI FILM CLASSICS

· ·

Rob White
SERIES EDITOR

Edward Buscombe, Colin MacCabe, David Meeker and Markku Salmi
SERIES CONSULTANTS

Launched in 1992, BFI Film Classics is a series of books that introduces, interprets and honours 360 landmark works of world cinema. The series includes a wide range of approaches and critical styles, reflecting the diverse ways we appreciate, analyse and enjoy great films.

Magnificently concentrated examples of flowing freeform critical poetry.
Uncut

A formidable body of work collectively generating some fascinating insights into the evolution of cinema.
Times Higher Education Supplement

The choice of authors is as judicious, eclectic and original as the choice of titles.
Positif

Estimable.
Boston Globe

We congratulate the BFI for responding to the need to restore an informed level of critical writing for the general cinephile.
Canadian Journal of Film Studies

Well written, impeccably researched and beautifully presented ... as a publishing venture, it is difficult to fault.
Film Ireland

FORTHCOMING IN 2002

· ·

The Blue Angel
S. S. Prawer

I Know Where I'm Going!
Pam Cook

The Manchurian Candidate
Greil Marcus

Mother India
Gayatri Chatterjee

D1210469

BFI FILM
CLASSICS

VERTIGO

. . . .

Charles Barr

 Publishing

First published in 2002 by the
BRITISH FILM INSTITUTE
21 Stephen Street, London W1T 1LN

The British Film Institute
promotes greater understanding
and appreciation of, and
access to, film and moving image
culture in the UK.

British Library Cataloguing-in-Publication Data
A catalogue record for this book is available from the British Library

ISBN 0–85170–918–4

Series design by
Andrew Barron & Collis Clements Associates

Typeset in Fournier and Franklin Gothic by
D R Bungay Associates, Burghfield, Berks

Printed in Great Britain by Cromwell Press, Trowbridge, Wiltshire

CONTENTS

· ·

ACKNOWLEDGMENTS
. . . .

My first debt is to the Research Committee of the place where I work, the University of East Anglia's School of English and American Studies, for a generous travel grant that enabled me to visit Los Angeles and San Francisco. Los Angeles is the location of the Margaret Herrick Library, a division of AMPAS (Academy of Motion Picture Arts and Sciences), whose many Special Collections include those of Alfred Hitchcock and of Paramount Pictures. I am grateful to the Special Collections Librarian, Scott Curtis, and to his colleagues at this user-friendly institution, for their help in giving me quick access to a wide range of *Vertigo* material. In San Francisco, Jim Kitses provided support and local knowledge, and Jill Brooke gave me a superbly efficient tour of the main *Vertigo* locations.

For various other kinds of help and advice, I am grateful to Justine Ashby, Ian Christie, Sam Cobb, Pam Cook, Leo Enticknap, Lisle Foote, Sid Gottlieb, Sheldon Hall, Steve Marchant, Danny Nissim, Alex Noel-Tod, Denis Norden, David Pirie, Ginette Vincendeau and Rob White. I especially thank Sergio Angelini for an early loan of his copy of the U.S. laserdisc edition of the film.

OBSESSION

....

'It's one of the most stunning entrances in all of cinema': Edward
Buscombe wrote this of John Wayne in *Stagecoach*, in the very first
sentence of the first book in this BFI Film Classics series.[1] Equally
stunning is the entrance of Kim Novak in *Vertigo*.

It is an entrance of a very different kind. 'We hear a shot, and cut
suddenly to Ringo standing by the trail, twirling his rifle. "Hold it", cries
the unmistakable voice of John Wayne. The camera dollies quickly
in ...'. Wayne is male, active, vocal, about to impose himself forcefully
on the narrative. Novak is female, passive, silent, offering herself as an
object to the male gaze.

The gaze is that of Scottie, a retired detective, played by James
Stewart. An old college acquaintance, Gavin Elster, has asked him to trail
his wife, Madeleine, who has been acting mysteriously. Scottie is
reluctant, but agrees to come that evening to the restaurant, Ernie's,
where the couple are dining, in order to have a discreet look at her. An
establishing shot of the restaurant exterior is followed by a close shot of
Scottie at the bar, looking intently over his shoulder into the space of the
room.

The obvious way to develop this would be to satisfy our curiosity
by cutting at once to his point of view, and an image of Madeleine. But we
are, with Scottie, kept waiting. First, the camera pulls back from his face,
and leftwards, in a smooth movement that loses him from the right of the

Scottie strains to get his first view of Madeleine ...

frame, and takes up a central vantage point on the dining room. It pauses, as if hesitating, then begins slowly to move in; at the same moment, a romantic musical theme begins also, reinforcing the sumptuousness both of the camera movement and of the décor, the dominant colours of which are deep red and blue and gold. The inward movement centres a particular table, at which we recognise Gavin Elster, with a blonde woman, who must be Madeleine: we see her from behind, her elegant black and turquoise outfit leaving her back exposed.

Only now do we return to Scottie, and then to his point of view as the couple, deep in the frame, start to get up and move towards where he is sitting. A pattern of alternation develops, cutting between him and his view of them, until Madeleine pauses, in profile, in front of him, so close to him that he has, in the next shot, to turn away, towards the bar, to avoid the danger of attracting her attention – or is it also that he is dazzled, blinded, by her beauty? Alternate close-ups continue, as she waits for her coat and he looks away. Only when she and Elster walk away from him to the exit is he free to resume his gaze.

Dissolve to Scottie at the wheel of his parked car, waiting for her to come out of her apartment the next day, so that he can follow her. He has, then, taken the job, and we don't need to be told that he has done so, or why. His first look at her has been decisive.

He is not the only one to be captivated. The scene has also indulged, in a pointed way, two other forms of gaze. First, that of the camera/director, in the voluptuously elaborate shot that first discovered Madeleine. Second, that of the audience: when Scottie has to look away, we are privileged to go on looking at Madeleine in close-up, in unobserved impunity. Of course these three kinds of look, those of director, character and audience, commonly go together in narrative cinema; one of the founding documents of modern film theory, Laura Mulvey's 'Visual Pleasure and Narrative Cinema', is based on precisely this point.[2] The mechanism of the point-of-view (POV) shot allows director and spectator to enjoy the same voyeuristic gaze at the female that the male hero does; for both, the character acts as a kind of surrogate. It is no surprise that Mulvey uses as the prime illustration of her thesis the director of *Vertigo*, Alfred Hitchcock, supreme manipulator of POV structures. 'In Hitchcock ... the male hero does see precisely what the audience sees.' This is true of much of *Vertigo*, but not of the crucial scene that introduces Madeleine, which so deftly separates out the three looks of voyeuristic fascination – those of director/camera, then character, then audience – as if to insist that 'we are all in this together'. And then, the next day, Scottie starts trailing her, and the classic three-in-one mechanism clicks into place, and continues with an intensity that can have few if any parallels in the history of cinema: lengthy sequences where Scottie follows Madeleine and we see, in a hypnotically protracted alternation of shots, exactly the images of her that he sees. It is not until nearly 30 minutes after her entry into the film that we and Scottie will hear her speak, and 20 of those minutes have been devoted to Scottie's trailing of her.

This pattern is at the root of what is special about *Vertigo*. It draws in, and indulges, the pleasurable gaze with extraordinary fullness, and at the same time foregrounds the mechanisms behind it – first by taking them apart, then by pushing them to an extreme. Indeed the plot, when fully revealed, will turn out to foreground these mechanisms still more decisively at the level of narrative, hinging as it does on the discovery that the entire scenario of surveillance has been a devious construction, set up by Gavin Elster with Madeleine's connivance and with Scottie as victim. Kim Novak is not simply, as a first viewing suggests, playing for Hitchcock the role of a woman being voyeuristically observed; she is playing, for Hitchcock, the part of a woman who is playing, for Elster, the part of a woman being voyeuristically observed. Absorbing at first viewing, when we don't know the full plot, these scenes become even more so when overlaid by the bittersweet awareness that, with Scottie, we have been, and are now again allowing ourselves to be, led on, deceived, by a consummate manipulator, complaisant victims of what has all along been – like all cinema – an illusory construction. If at one level Hitchcock = Scottie = spectator, it is plausible, and by no means incompatible, also to align Hitchcock and Elster, as directors of the calculated apparatus of illusion to which Scottie and the viewer are submitted. (It is an index of Hitchcock's concern for the precise management of the 'look' in this scene at Ernie's that he tinkered with it at the last minute, as recalled by Associate Producer Herbert Coleman in the laserdisc edition of the film. In the script, as Madeleine waits to exit the restaurant, 'Her eyes come to rest on Scottie for a moment', and it was shot this way, but Hitchcock then decided that this might risk giving a premature hint to audiences of the trap that was being laid. He therefore substituted another shot of her

Elster 'directs' Scottie

head turning, directed by Coleman during Hitchcock's absence on holiday in Jamaica. The original shot can be glimpsed in the film's trailer, prefixed to the video release of the restored version.)

We are, indeed, 'all in it together', director and cast, characters and viewers, caught up in the beautiful illusory construction. This story of a man who develops a romantic obsession with the image of an enigmatic woman has commonly been seen, by his colleagues as well as by critics and biographers, as one that engaged Hitchcock in an especially profound way; and it has exerted a comparable fascination on many of its viewers. After first seeing it as a teenager in 1958, Donald Spoto had gone back for 26 more viewings by the time he wrote *The Art of Alfred Hitchcock* in 1976.[3] In a 1996 magazine article, Geoffrey O'Brien cites other cases of 'permanent fascination' with *Vertigo*, and then casually reveals that he himself, starting at age 15, has seen it 'at least thirty times'.[4] No other film has inspired such a flow of pilgrims to its locations. Spoto's book records perhaps the first such systematic pilgrimage; writing for the *San Francisco Magazine* in 1982, Lynda Myles and Michael Goodwin anatomised and recommended the '*Vertigo* Tour', and countless fans have followed that tour since, as I did myself in 1997 (how else could I have presumed to write this book?).[5]

All this obsessiveness has been intensified by the elusive status of the film itself. It soon became hard to see it in a good print; in England at least, after its initial release, its most frequent screenings were in 16mm library prints, in black and white only. Then it became hard to see it at all, anywhere. The rights to *Vertigo*, as to four other features – *Rope*, *Rear Window*, *The Trouble with Harry*, and the second version of *The Man Who Knew Too Much* – reverted to the Hitchcock estate, which withheld them for more than a decade, on either side of Hitchcock's death in 1980. Like Myles and Goodwin, I have vivid memories of a one-off screening in 1981, in Norfolk rather than, in their case, California, laid on, illicitly of course, by a collector. We gazed at the film with the intentness of Scottie gazing at Madeleine, not knowing if we would ever see it again, ever truly possess it. Then, along with the other four titles, it was re-released in 1983, and widely re-reviewed. But even when this was followed by video release, the special aura around the film was not dispelled: a restoration was in progress, with the goal of recapturing the visual and aural splendour of the original production in VistaVision ('Motion Picture High Fidelity', a format that the film industry has not persevered with). It was as if Hitchcock, from beyond the grave, was manipulating his audience once again: giving, withholding, making us wait, and finally again gratifying us. And so, in 1996 (America) and 1997 (England), *Vertigo* was once more re-released and re-reviewed. For a film nearly 40 years old, its box-office performance was remarkable, and the critical response was in line with the high status accorded it in the most recent of the ten-yearly international polls of critics and film-makers conducted by *Sight and Sound* magazine; in 1992 it was ranked fourth, behind three older films, Ozu's *Tokyo Story* (third), Renoir's *La Règle du jeu* (second), and, in top place, the inevitable *Citizen Kane*.[6]

Yet on its first release in 1958 the public and critical reception of *Vertigo* had been less than enthusiastic. In a survey of the initial reaction of American critics, Robert E. Kapsis notes that while it 'generated a wide spectrum of critical response', the reviews in the 'more prestigious' weekly and monthly journals, from *Newsweek* to *The Saturday Review*, were generally hostile, John McCarten's verdict in *The New Yorker* being typical: 'Alfred Hitchcock, who produced and directed the thing, has never before indulged in such far-fetched nonsense.'[7] In England, the reception was if anything rather less friendly. Of the 28 newspaper and magazine reviews that I have looked at, six are, with reservations, favourable, nine are very mixed, and 13 almost wholly negative. Common to all of these reviews is a lack of sympathy with the basic structure and drive of the picture. Even the friendlier ones single out for praise elements that seem, from today's perspective, to be marginal virtues and incidental pleasures – the 'vitality' of the supporting performances (Dilys Powell in *The Sunday Times*), the slickness with which the car sequences are put together (Isobel Quigley in *The Spectator*).

Two years later, Hitchcock would again get a mixed reception for *Psycho*, alienating some critics more severely than he had ever done before. 'I grew so sick and tired of the beastly business that I didn't stop to see the ending', wrote C. A. (Caroline) Lejeune, a former friend and champion of his, in *The Observer*. Earlier that year she had applied the identical adjective to a British film directed by Michael Powell: 'It's a long time since a film disgusted me as much as *Peeping Tom*. ... I don't propose to name the players in this beastly picture.'[8]

This is a reminder of the affinity between the two greatest of English directors, and of the striking pattern of parallels and divergences between their careers. Six years younger than Hitchcock, Powell worked with him for a time in the late 1920s, notably on *Blackmail* (1929). A decade later, both men had a career-defining reorientation: while Hitchcock was negotiating the contract with David O. Selznick that took him to Hollywood, Powell was beginning the contract with Alexander Korda that introduced him to his long-term script collaborator, Emeric Pressburger. Equally single-minded in his commitment to cinema, equally opposed to the realist aesthetic, and inclined now and then to sign his films with a cameo appearance, Powell is, in a sense, the Hitchcock who didn't go to Hollywood; his concept of the 'composed film' is comparable with Hitchcock's concept of 'pure cinema'.

Peeping Tom and *Psycho* have much in common. Shot in late 1959, on low budgets, they centre on likeable young men who have been emotionally crippled in childhood and become serial killers, and they offered similar challenges to censors and to critics through their graphic portrayal of violence against women and of twisted sexuality. But the parallels between *Peeping Tom* and *Vertigo* are, while less obvious, in some ways even stronger. Hitchcock disarmed criticism of *Psycho* by insisting, with whatever depths of deviousness, that it was meant as a joke; Powell never took that line on *Peeping Tom*, nor did Hitchcock ever belittle the seriousness of *Vertigo*. Both are intensely romantic films, ending in a

paroxysm of love and death that leaves the surviving partner (Anna Massey, James Stewart), and the spectator alongside them, shattered, with nothing left to cling on to. And the critical standing of both films has changed dramatically over the years, more so even than that of *Psycho*; both have gone from derided or patronised failure to achieve a secure central place in academic film study and in the critical literature. Produced in a period of major changes in the film industry and also in film culture, they were ahead of their time, but their time duly came.

They were not the kind of material calculated to appeal to the Anglo-Saxon critical establishment that was still dominant at the end of the 1950s, committed as it was to common-sense notions of realism and social responsibility, and distrustful of commerce and fantasy. A full-page still from *Vertigo* was used in the Autumn 1960 issue of *Sight and Sound* to illustrate an article by Richard Roud on the excesses of film criticism in France, where it had been rated as one of the best films of its year, alongside the work of even more surprising figures like Douglas Sirk and Sam Fuller; a recent book by Claude Chabrol and Eric Rohmer had described Hitchcock as 'one of the greatest inventors of forms in the history of the cinema'.[9] 'One's first reaction' to all this, Roud suggested, 'might be to conclude that these men must be very foolish', though he went on to acknowledge that the early films of the *nouvelle vague* of which these two were part did not seem to be the work of fools.[10] In the event, the departure at this time of Lejeune as the *Observer* film critic after 30 years was only one element in a much wider transformation of film culture then getting unstoppably under way, of which the progressive revaluation of Hitchcock and, rather later, Powell, was a central and symptomatic part.

Both *Peeping Tom* and *Vertigo* preface their narratives with the extreme close-up of an eye, as if to announce at once the themes of vision and subjectivity. In *Peeping Tom* we can detect, below the closed lid, the rapid eye movement that denotes dreaming; the eye thereupon opens wide, introducing a story that has the intensity and condensed logic of dream, or nightmare. As *Vertigo*'s credits begin, the camera moves across the face of an unidentified woman. After first framing the mouth, it moves up to a close-up of the right eye, which opens wide, as if in shock; then moves further in, as if into its interior depths, from which galaxy-like spirals emerge. The spirals evoke the universe, like the galaxies at the opening of an earlier Powell film, *A Matter of Life and Death* (1946), or

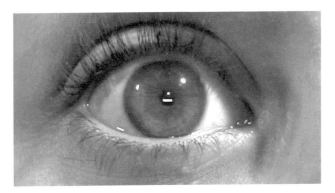

The eye in the opening credits

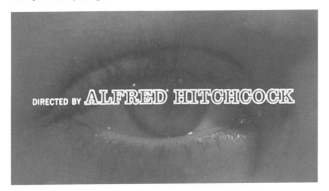

Hitchcock's credit

Hitchcock's cameo appearance

The eye at the beginning of *Peeping Tom*

Powell's credit

Powell's cameo appearance

the immense heaven discovered, at the same film's climax, behind David Niven's closing eyelid. This was not a film that Hitchcock was unaware of; when, in the course of preparing it, Powell and Pressburger visited Hollywood, it was he who entertained them and solved their casting problem by recommending Kim Hunter for the part of the American radio operator.[11] *A Matter of Life and Death* begins its narrative proper with a precipitous fall, presented with great vividness, which functions as both real and metaphorical: David Niven jumps from a blazing plane, with no parachute, survives miraculously, and at once *falls* in love – or rather, has already begun to do so, while talking by radio to Kim Hunter during the plane's descent, and the first sight of her confirms it. James Stewart's survival at the start of *Vertigo*, when, after the death-fall of his police colleague, he is left hanging by his fingertips from a gutter over a great height, seems, in naturalistic terms, equally improbable: as Robin Wood puts it, 'There seems no possible way he could have got down. The effect is of having him, throughout the film, metaphorically suspended over a great abyss.'[12] This metaphorical dimension is signalled in the film's title – insisted on by Hitchcock against Paramount's opposition – and in such details as the script directions for a scene in mid-film between Stewart and Novak, when he asks, 'Has this ever happened to you before, falling into San Francisco Bay?' In response, 'she looks relieved, for she had thought for a moment that he was going to say "falling in love"'.

These plays with metaphor and vision, these extraordinary moves between external and internal worlds, are typical of Powell and of Hitchcock and of the affinities between their forms of cinema. (Three films directed by Powell soon after *A Matter of Life and Death* end, as *Vertigo* will end, with a woman falling to her death: *Black Narcissus* (1947), *The Red Shoes* (1948), *Gone to Earth* (1950).) It's entirely consistent that the response of both of them to major changes in the institution of cinema, the breaking up in the 1950s of the old frameworks of production and reception, should have involved a comparably bold exploitation and exploration of the taken-for-granted mechanics of the gaze; the analysis set out in Mulvey's pioneering article of 1975 is already implicit in *Vertigo* and *Peeping Tom*, both in plots that are founded on a calculated male manipulation of the apparatus of looking, and in the shot-by-shot construction of key scenes. In *Peeping Tom*, with its killer-cameraman as protagonist, the analysis becomes not so much implicit as explicit, uncompromisingly so, leading to its now-notorious rejection by critics and distributors alike.[13] In contrast, however unappreciated *Vertigo* may have been at the time, it could be marketed even then with moderate success as a luxuriantly strange romantic thriller; and it did not take long for the high French valuation of Hitchcock, and especially of recent Hitchcock, to start to find echoes elsewhere.

In an essay on *Psycho* for an Oxford magazine in 1960, V. F. Perkins claimed that it was 'not just art – Hitchcock's genius guarantees that – but great art'. In 1965, in *Hitchcock's Films*, Robin Wood described *Vertigo* as 'Hitchcock's masterpiece to date, and one of the four or five most profound and beautiful films the cinema has yet given us'.[14] Great art, genius, masterpiece, profound and beautiful: the foregrounding of these words belongs to that polemical early period of English auteurism, in which the discovery and celebration of artists within Hollywood was both exciting in itself and, in helping to validate popular cinema as a legitimate field for critical and academic study, politically important. Accustomed as we are to an abundance of academic courses and publications on film, it takes an effort to recall that *Hitchcock's Films* was the first substantial director monograph of its kind to be published in English. A brilliant pioneer work, it helped set a new agenda for the study of Hollywood cinema. In a series of subsequent writings, Wood has revised and refined his account of Hitchcock's work and status, thus both responding to, and contributing to, wider ongoing debates about what is important in cinema, and in the study and analysis of cinema. For him and others, *Vertigo* has continued to be a major reference point. Jonathan Coe observes that 'like many of the very greatest films, *Vertigo* is open – and has been subjected – to a variety of different interpretations'.[15] Susan White elaborates this: in the years since it became widely available, *Vertigo* has been analysed by a wide range of critics as

> a tale of male aggression and visual control; as a map of the female Oedipal trajectory; as a deconstruction of the male construction of femininity and of masculinity itself; as a stripping bare of the mechanisms of directorial, Hollywood studio and colonial oppression; and as a place where textual meanings play out in an infinite regress of self-reflexivity.[16]

That is a formidable catalogue, and it is not hard to make fun of its pretensions; indeed on the basis of this quote alone Peter Conrad, in *The*

Hitchcock Murders, disingenuously writes off the whole business of Hitchcock scholarship as a self-serving waste of time.[17] This is not the place to try to mount an adequate commentary in opposition, discriminating between the obscurantist and the enlightening among the dizzying range of writings that *Vertigo* has inspired; it is more realistic to ask just what it is about *Vertigo* that gives it this *Hamlet*-like status as such an exceptionally fascinating and fertile text. When Sam Taylor, one of the two credited writers, was asked about its deeper meanings, he emphasised his and Hitchcock's concern with the mechanics of the story: 'Hitchcock was all for what he called the "yarn". It's a nice little English word – he said "that's a good yarn".'[18] Another key pragmatic term that Hitchcock often dwelt on was the 'icebox' factor. People get home from seeing a film, and talk over key points in the story as they raid the refrigerator for a late-night snack; it should be constructed solidly enough for them not to feel cheated, and intriguingly enough for them to think of going back to check these key points out.[19] *Vertigo* is indeed 'a good yarn', with a particularly strong icebox factor. It is precisely because it is such a remarkable mechanism, both on the 'yarn' level of the narrative and in its shot-by-shot construction, that it is able to invite and support so many readings.

CONSTRUCTION
. . . .

Robert Carringer's study of *Citizen Kane* and its production opens with these words: '"It is, above all, the creation of one man". That pronouncement on *Citizen Kane* by an early critic set the terms on which discussion of the film would be centered for decades to come.'[20] There is an echo here of what Hitchcock had written as early as 1927: 'when moving pictures are really artistic they will be created entirely by one man'.[21] Most writers on Hitchcock and *Vertigo*, including those to whom Susan White's catalogue implicitly refers, continue in effect to write as though Hitchcock had fulfilled this aspiration, even if they pay lip-service to the need to go beyond auteurism. Carringer, in contrast, goes on to argue convincingly that '*Citizen Kane* is not only Hollywood's greatest film, but it is also, I contend, Hollywood's single most successful instance of collaboration. In a very real sense, the two propositions are synonymous.'[22] I believe this is a valid perspective for looking at *Vertigo*, and indeed at Hitchcock's work more widely.

Take the restaurant scene already described, which is crucial in generating the main emotional and narrative dynamic of the film. Hitchcock asked for the exact recreation, on a Hollywood sound-stage, of the upmarket San Francisco restaurant Ernie's. In producing a replica as convincing in ambience as it is in dimensions, and so sumptuously inhabited, he depended on skills of art direction (Hal Pereira and Henry Bumstead), costuming (Edith Head), hairstyling (Nellie Manley), and make-up (Wally Westmore); to realise those very precise and intense colour compositions, he leaned heavily on his director of photography (Robert Burks) and camera operator (Leonard South); to fine-tune the sequence of 15 shots, he used a skilled editor (George Tomasini). And even if we decide to count these skills as essentially artisanal rather than creative, skills that simply (!) enabled the perfect physical realisation of a film that was already playing in Hitchcock's mind – and even if we also put on one side the contribution of actors – there are two areas where others had an input that by any definition was creative: music and script.

Bernard Herrmann, who constitutes the common factor between *Vertigo* and *Kane*, evidently used to claim that, when they worked together, Hitchcock left his films only 60 per cent complete: the remaining 40 per cent was provided by his music.[23] Though the percentage figure may be disputed, it remains incontestable that *Vertigo*, like its two successors, *North by Northwest* and *Psycho*, would be less powerfully affecting without the Herrmann score, and that Herrmann was doing more than, as it were, simply making up a prescription that Hitchcock had written out. The entry of his beautiful romantic theme, at the moment we first become aware of Madeleine in the restaurant, is integral to the scene's mesmerising effect.

The scene belongs to an intricate narrative structure that took more than a year to work out on paper through a succession of drafts. Elsewhere, I have argued for the importance of a range of writers in helping, in the formative English years of his career, actually to create the template for what we now identify as the Hitchcock film, notably the two who have script credit on a long succession of the silent and early sound films respectively, Eliot Stannard and Charles Bennett.[24] Even as late as *Vertigo*, for all the experience and authority he had by then accumulated – 'the power and the freedom', in the words of the *Vertigo* script itself – Hitchcock could seem helpless without a clear guiding hand.

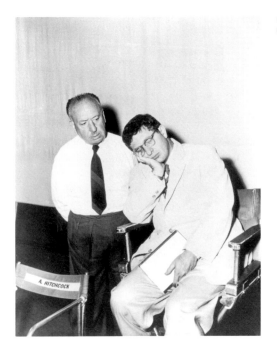

Hitchcock at Bernard
Herrmann's shoulder

It was in the mid-1950s that he had started to become truly a household name. Not only was his fame as a film-maker secure after a decade and a half in Hollywood, but his image became widely disseminated through the TV show bearing his name, which he produced, occasionally directed and always quirkily fronted: opening in October 1955, it ran through nine successive annual seasons, 266 shows in all, until March 1965. His work in this decade falls into two very different categories. The TV films were short, quickly turned out, black-and-white and visually simple, based on a single idea, with some kind of macabre and/or joky twist ending; the stories he directed himself were no exception. The cinema films, in contrast, became increasingly elaborate: thematically complex, with high production values, generally in colour, meticulously prepared over a long period.

This diagram is over-simple, to the extent that TV elements did seep into Hitchcock's movie-making. This was in line with industry trends: while Hollywood's right hand made ever more spectacular films in the new big-screen formats, its left hand made a number of modest, realistic dramas in black and white, based or modelled on TV originals. The key film here is *Marty*, 1956 Oscar-winner, from the celebrated play broadcast live in 1953 by NBC; Kim Novak, soon after *Vertigo*, would make the austere, unglamorous *Middle of the Night* (1959), another transposition of a TV play by the writer/director team from *Marty*, Paddy Chayefsky and Delbert Mann. Hitchcock interspersed his own exotic colour projects with the downbeat and self-consciously realistic *The Wrong Man* (1956), and then with *Psycho* (1960) – thematically far beyond TV's range, but black-and-white, low-budget, and shot on a tight schedule by the same crew that he used for the TV show.

While *Vertigo*, filmed in the new VistaVision process, clearly belongs in the exotic colour spectacular category, it is in some ways closer, in terms of source material and plot outline, to the model of his TV series than any film he had previously made: based on a grim form of practical joke, it has an abrupt 'twist' ending, and one of its two credited scriptwriters is Alec Coppel, whose stories would form the basis for several of the Hitchcock TV shows both before and after *Vertigo*'s release.

The story of the film's production has now been thoroughly documented by Dan Auiler.[25] Having been through much of the same archival material that he uses, I can attest to his book's scholarly accuracy, which enables me gratefully to compress my own account of the production process; it should be read alongside this.

The basis of *Vertigo* is a short novel by Pierre Boileau and Thomas Narcejac, *D'entre les morts* (*From among the Dead*), first published in French in 1954.[26] This pair always wrote in tandem, specialised in noir suspense thrillers and were at their most successful around this time; they scripted Georges Franju's poetic horror film *Les Yeux sans visage* (*Eyes without a Face*, 1960), while on British television ATV's *Armchair Theatre* series used two adaptations from their work in its 1958 season, around the time *Vertigo* was seen in cinemas.[27] Hitchcock had shown an interest in two of their previous novels, *Le Salaire de la peur* (*The Wages of Fear*) and *Les Diaboliques* (*The Fiends*), but both were acquired by the French director Henri-Georges Clouzot, and the international success of the resulting films led some critics to bracket the two men together as experts in the suspense genre. Possibly this put Hitchcock on his mettle, and made him determined not to lose out to Clouzot a third time; at any rate, he announced the Boileau–Narcejac adaptation as a project even before it appeared in English translation, three years before filming would actually begin.

Despite what Hitchcock used to say about his cavalier strategy for adapting novels ('What I do is to read a story only once, and if I like the basic idea, I just forget all about the book and start to create cinema'), this adaptation would stay close to the structure of the original.[28] The following plot synopsis covers both novel and film:

A retired detective is hired by an old college acquaintance to keep an eye on his wife. The detective left the force after an attack of acrophobia which caused a colleague to fall to his death. The wife is apparently possessed by the spirit of her great-grandmother, who committed suicide.

Once he sees her, the man becomes fascinated, accepts the commission, saves her from drowning, falls in love. But when she runs compulsively to the top of a high building, his acrophobia stops him from following, and he is traumatised by the sight of a second death fall.

Time passes. Despite medical treatment, the man is haunted by her memory. Then he seems to find her again, in a lookalike: a woman from a quite different background who expresses bewilderment and then anger at his fixation on the first woman but is sufficiently drawn to him not to break off the romance developing between them. She even allows him to 'make her over' to look more like the original.

In fact, she is the same woman – not the wife of the college acquaintance, but his (then) mistress. She collaborated in his plot to kill the wife, by pretending to be her. The detective could be relied upon not to be able to climb to the top of the high building; the body that fell from the building was that of the wife, for whose apparent suicide he therefore took the moral blame.

He starts to realise the truth when the lookalike carelessly reveals that she possesses some distinctive jewellery that belonged to the first woman. His rage at unravelling the plot and discovering her duplicity leads, this time, to her death.

Even though this outline would remain, significant changes were necessary.

1.   A shift of setting from Paris to San Francisco.
2.   An updating in time: the novel spans the four years from early World War II to the liberation, and connections are made between the personal and public spheres which wouldn't work in terms of wartime America, even if Hitchcock had wanted the bother of a period setting, which he generally avoided.
3.   The formal shift from novel to film narrative, and specifically that of a high-budget Hollywood film, and a Hitchcock film. A cast of at best somewhat drab characters had to become more sympathetic and more glamorous; a fantastic plot had, without losing its fantastic quality, to be made as tight, logical and convincing as possible, in order to hold a mass cinema audience.

In Hitchcock's words, this presented a 'complicated construction problem'.[29] As usual, he turned to a playwright to help him, following the principle he would explain to Truffaut that 'a playwright will tend to make a better screenwriter than a novelist because he is used to the building of successive climaxes'.[30] By the time the script was complete, he would have got through three of them: Maxwell Anderson, Alec Coppel and Sam Taylor.

Of the three, Anderson was the oldest (at 68), the most celebrated for his stage work and the least committed to cinema, though he had a joint script credit for Hitchcock's preceding film *The Wrong Man*. He worked on adapting the novel during Hitchcock's absence abroad, and submitted a treatment in September 1956 with the Keatsian title *Darkling I Listen*. Donald Spoto describes it as incomprehensible, but it makes reasonable sense; it just doesn't seem at all promising as a blueprint.[31] Apart from the San Francisco setting, the use of a Mission Dolores location, and a structure based on three falls from a high place (as against the two falls in the book, which ends with a strangling), nothing would survive into the final film. Hitchcock acknowledged the need for a fresh start by hiring Alec Coppel.

Coppel was a British playwright, now under contract to Paramount, who had accumulated ten screen credits over two decades, and been nominated for an Oscar for the 1953 Alec Guinness comedy *The Captain's Paradise* (directed by Anthony Kimmins). Hitchcock at once took him on a tour of likely San Francisco locations. Once Coppel had got the feel of the story, there followed a series of script conferences in October and November 1956, the results of which he consolidated into a patchwork document of 50 scenes, completed in early December. This lays out the story without dialogue, but often in great descriptive detail. When this was complete, Coppel spent several more weeks, before other commitments took him away, in developing this script, putting in what Hitchcock described as 'dummy dialogue', most of it purely indicative and functional, a guide for later development. Meanwhile, Hitchcock turned again to Anderson and sent him, on 4 December, the new script, accompanied by a long and careful letter, which Auiler quotes almost in full; it explains the new concept and framework of the film in some detail, and invites Anderson, who was still under contract, to write the dialogue proper.[32]

Essentially, this is how Hitchcock seemed to like to operate: working out a firm linear construction in collaboration with a scenarist, preferably one from a theatre background, and then using the same writer, or a fresh one, to fill out the dialogue; see the vivid accounts given, in interview, by his major British collaborator of the sound period, Charles Bennett, who saw himself as an expert 'constructionist' rather than as a dialogue man.[33] The intention was, it seems, for Coppel's script to be adopted, when complete, as the definitive blueprint, subject to embellishments by Anderson, had it not been for a set of unforeseen developments.

Despite Hitchcock's attempt at tact, Anderson pulled out. In his place, in mid-January 1957, a third playwright was brought in, Sam Taylor. It seems that he was being asked, in the event, to do rather more than fill in the dialogue, since the Coppel script was felt, notably by James Stewart, to be still somewhat mechanical, lacking in believable characters.[34] In any case, the very next day after Taylor's arrival, Hitchcock was rushed to hospital for a hernia operation. Before fully recovering, he was readmitted in early March for a second operation, this time for the removal of a gallstone. In effect, with Hitchcock ill and Anderson and Coppel no longer involved, Taylor was able to take the script over. After delivering his revised version in early April, he returned in May for three more weeks' work, and the result, after consultations with Hitchcock, would go forward with little change to constitute the final script, dated 12 September 1957.

The next day, Hitchcock sent a copy of this script to Coppel, along with a letter which is, by all accounts, typical of his style: 'Personally I hate getting involved in the question of credits, etc., but naturally I would, of course, like everyone to be happy ... Unfortunately, Samuel Taylor has requested a solo screenplay credit. I don't know how strongly you feel about this ...' Replying on 16 September, Coppel turned out to feel strongly enough to insist on going to arbitration. Paramount's Story Editor therefore wrote to the Writers' Guild of America on 1 October, enclosing copies of all script materials and asking for an adjudication. Their verdict was that the credit should read: 'Screenplay by Alec Coppel and Samuel Taylor', and this is the formula used on screen.

Most subsequent accounts have suggested that this was an injustice to Taylor, based on some kind of contractual technicality. Coppel died in 1972, but Taylor lived until 1999, gave many interviews in response to the growth of interest in the film and its director, and came to talk as if he had in fact earned the right to sole credit. The two standard Hitchcock biographies take the same line, stating that Hitchcock abandoned Coppel's work altogether and had Taylor start again from scratch. This is far from the truth. It is no disparagement of Taylor's input to claim that Coppel, who remains the one prominently credited contributor to have had no attention whatever on the occasion of any of *Vertigo*'s successive releases, deserves some posthumous rehabilitation.[35]

In fact, the fortuitous Coppel–Taylor pairing suited the project exceptionally well. Coppel was the kind of neat constructionist whose stories were, as noted earlier, good material for the Hitchcock TV show. His most interesting pre-*Vertigo* screen credit is for a 1949 film directed in London by Edward Dmytryk, and released in the US as *The Hidden Room*; he wrote the script from his own novel, and acted as dialogue director. The British title for it is *Obsession* – a potential title for *Vertigo*, and the very title that Paul Schrader and Brian de Palma would use for their self-conscious homage to *Vertigo* in 1975, complete with a Bernard Herrmann score. The 1949 *Obsession* is centred on a man who, Elster-like, concocts an elaborate plot against his wife, and his chosen means, murdering her lover in an acid bath, shows how much Coppel was in tune with some of Hitchcock's own more gruesome interests. Likewise, the barbed, sardonic lines he writes for Naunton Wayne's Scotland Yard man suggest Taylor was wrong to claim, years after Coppel's death, that only Hitchcock himself could have written the coroner's speech for the inquest, which is already there, more or less as shot, in the pre-Taylor script.[36] A study of this script and accompanying memoranda show how much of Coppel's work survives into the final film. In his letter of 4 December to Anderson, Hitchcock wrote that 'Mr Alec Coppel ... has been of tremendous assistance in helping me to unravel the complicated construction problem of *From among the Dead*', which by his grudging standards is high praise. Along with much of the detail, the basic narrative is already there: a fantastic plot mechanism, skilfully incorporating a number of emotionally charged 'big scenes' of the kind which Hitchcock habitually started by conceiving, but needing to be fleshed out further.

This is where Taylor came in. As a playwright, he was best-known for his authorship of the romantic comedy *Sabrina*, and as co-author of the adaptation filmed by Billy Wilder in 1954.[37] Sabrina, played in the film by Audrey Hepburn, is manipulated by the wealthy Larrabee brothers, who enjoy 'the power and the freedom' to get their way both sexually and in business. Aware that his younger brother is in danger of being distracted by her from going through with an important dynastic marriage, Linus (Humphrey Bogart), head of the family firm, puts together a cold-blooded scheme to get Sabrina out of the way: he embarks on his own rival courtship of her, setting up a romantic trip for two to Paris. Once she has committed herself by catching the boat, he intends to abandon her and pay her off. In the event he fails to go through with it, first confessing the plot to her prematurely, and then realising that he genuinely returns her love. It will be evident that, like Coppel's *Obsession*, this has elements that made its author intelligent casting for *Vertigo*, being a yarn based on arrogant male exploitation, deception and unexpected love – told mainly from the woman's viewpoint, and incorporating a key scene of confession.

Taylor at once set to work on 'humanising' *Vertigo* by writing a new female character. There is no reason here to question his account:

> I told [Hitchcock] immediately that I would have to invent a character who would bring Scottie into the world, establish for him an ordinary life, make it obvious that he's an ordinary man. So I invented Midge ... Having made Midge, the whole thing fell into place, and if you think about the picture, you'll find that it wouldn't work well without her. It wouldn't be believable. All the Midge scenes were mine. I say this because in writing about Hitchcock all writers say they slavishly attended to him and discussed everything with him. I never had that experience. I told him I was going to create a character. He said, 'Fine'. I went off and created the character. It was as simple as that. He didn't know anything about Midge until he read the script and liked it.[38]

Midge appears in Taylor's first script, and his second and final one includes another new element, the confessional flashback which resolves the mystery for the audience 40 minutes from the end by revealing that Judy, the woman who intrigues Scottie by her resemblance to the Madeleine he has loved and lost, is in fact the same woman. We see, in flashback, the way Elster and Judy between them deceived Scottie, and we hear from Judy how her love for him has made her risk meeting him again. This scene has been one of the most discussed elements in *Vertigo*, and a number of claims have accumulated around it: that it alienated critics and audiences in 1958, and was a main cause of the film's initial failure; that it was, typically and brilliantly, the cornerstone of Hitchcock's basic concept for adapting the novel; that, even if it took a lot of work to evolve this structure, it is in retrospect the only truly 'Hitchcockian' one; and that it represents in principle an exceptionally bold and unusual strategy. Although none of these claims in fact stands up to examination, the scene remains a shrewd addition, both in giving us a dramatic switch to the woman's subjectivity, and in alleviating a structural problem that had preoccupied Coppel and Hitchcock throughout the earlier stages of scripting. Without the revelation, the script becomes oppressively weighed down at the end with retrospective material, an anguished going over of past events from a triple perspective. It not only has to dramatise Scottie's realisation of his deception, and Judy's realisation that he has realised it – and the intense emotions on both sides that flow from this – but must also ensure, at the same time, that the audience is, in turn, getting a clear enough realisation of this past deception, in all its details and implications, to be able to

Midge, created by Sam Taylor to represent an 'ordinary life'

The Madeleine who might have been: Vera Miles with James Stewart in *The Man Who Shot Liberty Valance*

follow and to empathise. The anxiety this was causing is evidenced in an extraordinary document by Coppel headed 'Confessions on Tower' and listing no fewer than 25 separate points of explanation: details of fact and motivation in the 'backstory' that would either be made explicit as the revelation unfolded, or be inferrable by audiences as they mentally pieced things together. Among other things, the revelation scene makes this process of understanding much more manageable, and it is hard now to conceive of *Vertigo* without it. Although I know of no surviving memoranda in which it was discussed, it is reasonable to assume that the idea came from Taylor rather than Hitchcock, given that a confession scene is pivotal to *Sabrina*, and that Hitchcock had worked for so long on the film without suggesting it – and indeed that he tried, as we will see, to cut the scene out of the release prints at the last minute.[39]

Hitchcock had, then, got full value from the successive and complementary inputs of two very different writers, as might not have happened if he had stayed healthy, which would have meant an earlier starting date – or, alternatively, if Anderson had not walked out. These were two apparent setbacks which turned out to work to the film's advantage, a third being the pregnancy of Vera Miles, which made her unavailable to play the female lead. The received account is that Hitchcock, to whom she was under personal contract, always intended to use her in the role, was upset by her pregnancy, and turned with reluctance to Kim Novak, but Auiler indicates that it may not have been so simple: he was already considering Novak, whom Paramount preferred anyway to a relative unknown.[40] However, Miles's casting, opposite Stewart, had been formally announced on 17 January, and one wonders how Hitchcock, with his horror of awkward scenes, could otherwise have gone back on that. It is scarcely possible now to visualise her in the role, not only because Novak is so sensational in it, but also because Miles herself would never thereafter play a character of remotely comparable glamour or mystique, least of all in the two subsequent films where she did get to play opposite James Stewart, *The FBI Story* (1959) and *The Man Who Shot Liberty Valance* (1962) – or indeed as Janet Leigh's sister in *Psycho*.

ILLUSION
. . . .

The depths of the eye behind the credits, the rooftop chase, the policeman's fall; Scottie hangs agonisingly from the gutter. I have already cited Robin Wood's comment of 1965: 'There seems no possible way he could have got down. The effect is of having him, throughout the film, metaphorically suspended over a great abyss.' This idea has been hugely influential, quoted by a range of later writers and used as a starting point for their own readings of what the film is really about. Among them is James F. Maxfield, who argues

> that *Vertigo* may best be regarded as an extended equivalent of Ambrose Bierce's story (and Robert Enrico's film) *An Occurrence at Owl Creek Bridge*: that everything after the opening sequence is the dream or fantasy of a dying man (it makes no difference whether the dream occurs while he hangs from the gutter, as he falls to the street, or when he lies dying on the pavement).[41]

Set in the American Civil War, Bierce's story starts with a man being hanged and narrates his fall, his miraculous-seeming escape and his return across country to his home and family – only to reveal at the end that he is hanging dead, and that these are thoughts that have gone through his mind in the final instant of his life. Hitchcock certainly knew the story, which was adapted for his TV show in 1959, with Robert Stevenson as director, thus predating the Enrico cinema version shown in 1962 as *Incident at Owl Creek*. What is more, the first of the *Vertigo* script revisions delivered by Taylor carries on its title page the startling words 'From among the Dead, or There'll Never Be Another You, by Samuel Taylor and Ambrose Bierce'. Unknown presumably to Maxfield, since he doesn't mention it, this playful inscription points to an affinity that goes deeper than any single structuring device.[42]

Bierce specialised in the short story, a form that Hitchcock liked to compare with film in terms of its narrative span, and he acknowledged, as did Hitchcock, a debt to Edgar Allan Poe. All three men were preoccupied by suspense, death and the uncanny, and the Poe who wrote that 'The death … of a beautiful woman is, unquestionably, the most poetical topic in the world' would surely have loved *Vertigo*. A story from the same Bierce collection as 'Owl Creek' is entitled 'The Man out of the

Nose'. The Nose is part of an old rocky terrace in the North Beach area of San Francisco, where a set of cave-like dwellings has the look of a human face; we may recall that Hitchcock's proposed title for his next film after *Vertigo* was *The Man in Lincoln's Nose* (Cary Grant on Mount Rushmore, in what became *North by Northwest*). Bierce's story centres on a man obsessed with the wife of another; he views her at the upstairs open window of her home; their eyes meet, and, startled, she loses her balance and falls to a gruesome death. The man passes a year in an asylum, then goes to live near the Mission Dolores, before moving to 'the Nose'; from there, he takes a daily walk to 'fix an intensely expectant gaze' on the fatal window before returning home disappointed. And the very next story in this volume, 'An Adventure at Brownville', ends with another Californian woman falling to her death, driven to it in some obscure way by an oppressive male ego. 'With the smile of an angel upon her lips and that look of terror in her beautiful eyes Eva Maynard sprang from the cliff and shot crashing into the tops of the pines below!' The combination of location, event and psychology in these stories is, to say the least, extremely evocative of *Vertigo*.

Whether or not Bierce had an influence on the concept of the film already worked out between Hitchcock and Coppel, it's evident from his title page that Taylor had him in mind as he reworked the script and supplied dialogue. Having spent many years himself in San Francisco, Taylor will have been well aware of Bierce as a man who was at the centre of the city's life in the key period of its transformation and growth, and as a writer who wove a whole series of uncanny stories around some of its landmarks: see for instance, in addition to 'The Man out of the Nose', 'One of Twins', with its encounters around Union Square. The square is the back-projected location for the bookshop in *Vertigo* run by Pop Leibel, to which Midge takes Scottie to help him investigate Madeleine's nineteenth-century obsessions; as an authority on, in her words, the 'gay old Bohemian days', Pop will know the real history of the place, such as 'who shot who on the Embarcadero in August 1879'. No one would have known such things better than Bierce, who was at that very date the editor of a San Francisco paper, the *Argonaut* (Leibel's bookshop is the Argosy), and who was also secretary of the Bohemian Club. He was even a close friend of Lillie Coit (middle name Hitchcock), whose 1929 legacy would finance the building of the tower that bears her name and that is prominent in the film both visually and in dialogue.

The Bierce influence would help to account for the film's intense and rather magical quality of rootedness: in the city and its environs, in its historical past and in the uncanny dimensions waiting to be explored within and around it. This is notably different from Hitchcock's habitually more simplistic attitude to settings, one based on ensuring that the audience is comfortably oriented by picking landmarks already familiar to them, and by naming key locations emphatically. In *The 39 Steps* (1935), for instance, we have on the one hand the London Palladium and the Forth Bridge, and on the other the Scottish estate of Alt-na-Sheallach, several times named to prepare us for important events that will take place there. *Vertigo* likewise offers the Golden Gate Bridge, the Missions, the repeated naming and use of Ernie's, and so on; but beyond this there is an unusually rich texture of topographical allusion, at two levels: visual and verbal. We see some evocative places that are not named, like the redwood forest, Union Square and the Palace of Fine Arts (the building by the lake where, late in the film, the couple walk in the sunshine). Conversely, the Presidio, the Western Addition, Fort Point, the Bar at the Top of the Mark, the Portals of the Past, the Coit Tower and the Embarcadero are among the places which are named, also to evocative effect, but which we either don't see, or see without, at the time, knowing their name. The external real world of San Francisco past and present is delineated with great precision, but in a mode that is at the opposite extreme from documentary. It can be a surprise to read, in interviews and publicity, about the pedantically precise concern Hitchcock often showed for surface realism, not just in factually based projects like *The Wrong Man* but in fantasies like *The Birds* (1963), where he had every school child in the location village of Bodega Bay photographed as a guide to the representation, and clothing, of the children in the film.[43] For *Vertigo* he commissioned precise recordings of the dimensions and contents of Ernie's, the flower shop (Podesta Baldocchi) and the clothes shop (Ransohoffs), in order to recreate them exactly in the studio. The more anchored they are in the real, the more convincingly the interior and exterior environs can add up to comprise an alternate world of subjectivity and dream, like the reassuringly known and familiar world of home and its surroundings that Bierce's soldier hallucinates in his dying moment on the scaffold.

The specific 'Owl Creek' idea proposed by Maxfield relates suggestively to Hitchcock's established modes of narrative. Many of his earlier films show a central character unconscious, or daydreaming, and develop the adventure narrative directly out of that moment, as if to hint that it is generated from the depths of the unconscious, playing out the character's inmost desires and anxieties. Think of Margaret Lockwood lapsing into unconsciousness at the start of the train journey in *The Lady Vanishes* (1938), or of Joan Fontaine in *Suspicion* (1941) daydreaming over photographs of a Cary Grant who then miraculously materialises at her window. More recently, *Rear Window* (1954) opened with a series of slowly moving shots which repeatedly link the outside world of the courtyard opposite, in early morning, to the back of the sweating,

L. B. Jefferies' feverish sleep at the start of *Rear Window*

Scottie hanging over the abyss at the start of *Vertigo*

sleeping head of L. B. Jefferies, as if to insist that this world is contained within the dreamer's mind.

The descent into the eye, the nightmare quality of the opening chase and fall, and the use of the same actor in James Stewart, all seem to align *Vertigo* strongly, from the start, with *Rear Window*'s mode of oneiric narrative. But it's less easy to pin down what kinds of inner tension the external narrative will be playing out. Stewart's problem in *Rear Window* is clearly signalled as being a fear of marriage, of the settling down that is both prefigured and symbolised by having a broken leg in plaster. We get concise information about the personal lives of the Lockwood and Fontaine characters in the two earlier films, providing a framework for the wish-fulfilling love affairs that will develop. The same is true of the Powell–Pressburger film referred to earlier, *A Matter of Life and Death*, whose opening is as strange and disorienting as *Vertigo*'s, but which tells us all we need to know about the David Niven character's relation to his parents at the same time that it points him in the direction of romance. All these films, then, have a clear and precise psychological framework, as do the celebrated quartet with which Hitchcock will follow *Vertigo*: *North by Northwest*, *Psycho*, *The Birds*, *Marnie*. *Vertigo* itself remains more mysterious, more poetic. All we get to know of Scottie's background is that he was once engaged to Midge, that he remains unattached, that he has independent means, and that his acrophobia means that he is now an ex-policeman. Unattached, independent, unemployed: this free-floating quality makes him a blank page for critics to write on, and an everyman for audiences to relate to.

. . . .

Nel mezzo del cammin di nostra vita,
Mi ritrovai per una selva oscura
Che la diretta via era smarrita

The opening lines of Dante's *Divine Comedy* place the narrator 'in the middle of the journey of our life', at the moment when he loses his way and finds himself in a dark wood. Both Jefferies in *Rear Window* and Scottie in *Vertigo* are likewise in mid-life, and have their progress interrupted with equal suddenness. Before a word of dialogue is spoken, we are given, in the most direct and economical terms, visual evidence of the regular life-path and of its interruption: Jeff's work as an action photographer, established by the apparatus and pictures that surround him, and now cut short by his broken leg, and Scottie's work chasing criminals, cut short by the onset of his acrophobia.

'Men, are you over 40? When you wake up in the morning do you feel tired and run down? Do you have that listless feeling?' The first words in *Rear Window* are those of an early-morning radio advertisement, heard from a nearby apartment while Jefferies still sleeps, as if to spell out what is troubling his subconscious. His immobility, explained in plot terms as the result of a crash, works also to symbolise the reduced mobility of middle age – a middle age that may be felt as actual, as impending or as psychological, the man's confinement evoking the pressures of domesticity, and, beyond this, the increasingly sedentary lifestyle of urban Western man in the mid-twentieth century.

Born in 1908, James Stewart certainly fits the 'over 40' persona, but to see the films as 'about' middle age would be too limiting. It is integral to Stewart's star persona, and integral also to the way in which this kind of star operates in cinema, that his age should seem fluid, and this helps make possible a wide range of interpretations of what happens to him in *Vertigo*.[44] For Robin Wood (1989 revision), the 'boyishness' that is an enduring aspect of the persona means that he can function as a son figure first to Midge and then, in the next scene, to Elster, as he starts on the process of personality formation that follows the symbolic birth trauma of the initial scene on the rooftop.[45] James F. Maxfield accepts Scottie as being, indeed, older than Midge (as Stewart is older, by 15 years, than Barbara Bel Geddes), but explains this in terms of his 'Owl Creek' reading: Scottie is inserting a remembered sweetheart, from some 15 years back, into his instant-of-death dream.[46] At times Scottie presents himself as even older, past it, saying to Elster that 'I'm supposed to be retired', and 'I never married' – the definitive past tense, like the last sentence of a newspaper obituary – and Jonathan Coe describes him in the hospital scene as 'looking old and fragile in his thin cardigan'.[47] In his last major film performance, for John Ford in *The Man Who Shot Liberty Valance* in 1962, Stewart, by now 54, will play a senator who is at least ten years older and, in a lengthy flashback that forms the main narrative, the same character in his twenties. In this respect *Vertigo* works rather like *Liberty Valance* without the flashback, evoking a life-span and its possibilities, with Stewart as a Dantesque everyman disturbed and challenged at a mid-life stage that is as much symbolic as literal.

In *Rear Window*, Jeff struggles to recapture the freedom of his active, travelling lifestyle, as the hunter-gatherer of news stories, against the pressures that close in on him. *Vertigo* likewise, after its immobilising event, shows us the man in the room with the woman, chafing at physical restraint and inactivity, and looking to work out a future that doesn't involve being sedentary and tied down. Scottie is in Midge's apartment, still convalescing, unmoved by her devotion to him ('there's only one man for me'). Reminding her that they were once engaged for three weeks, he smiles ruefully at the memory of 'the good old college days'. That line functions, for me, like the initial radio message of *Rear Window*, evoking a time, an 'elsewhere', of youthful activity, spontaneity and libido, in contrast to his run-down present self. He resists the prospect of years spent 'behind a desk, chairborne', but Midge insists that this is now 'where you belong', and she works hard throughout this long scene to get him to accept his condition. Her problem is that to do so is to acquiesce in his loss of virile energy, with all that this implies, so where does that leave her? Lisa in *Rear Window* had the same problem, which she solved, at least to some extent (the end is ambivalent), by encouraging her man to get his excitement through fantasy, indulging and then abetting his voyeuristic absorption in the narratives across the courtyard; and her triumph was to actually insert herself into that exciting screen/fantasy narrative, by crossing over to participate. But she was the star, Grace Kelly, rather than a self-effacingly deglamorised supporting player; and when Midge, later, tries a comparable kind of cross-over, painting herself into a new version of the romantic portrait that fascinates Scottie, the result will be disaster.

Vertigo still has its female star to come. Scottie's route to her, away from the room and Midge and the threat of the desk job, is linked, in a skilful piece of writing, to the memory of the 'good old college days' and the more active life it represents. Mentioning those days reminds him that a long-lost college contemporary has phoned and wants to see him: Gavin Elster.

The next scene in Elster's office – preceded by an exterior shot, through which Hitchcock and Scottie walk in different directions – is similar in structure to the one at Midge's place. Both scenes are expository, constructing character and situation and setting up what follows. Both are very talky, photographed mainly in separate, alternating shots, with the characters occasionally framed together, whether to establish space clearly or for dramatic and psychological nuance. Both scenes have a 'false ending' a little after halfway, with Scottie making to leave the room, and then deciding after all to prolong the conversation. With Midge, he pauses on his way out to ask what she meant by saying his acrophobia was incurable; she admits to having exaggerated her doctor's verdict, and he stays to try to show that he can beat it. Then, when Elster pleads with him to follow his wife Madeleine, to find out where she goes when in her tranced state, evidently possessed in some way by a figure from the past, he at first refuses. At the door, he again pauses, not wishing to seem impolite, and allows himself to be drawn back in, as he has to do if Elster's plot, and the film's plot, are to go forward. So in each scene he is drawn, half-reluctantly, by second thoughts or inner compulsion, into something active, non-chairborne, potentially dangerous.

Agreeing to come to the restaurant where Elster and Madeleine will be dining, Scottie murmurs its name: 'Ernie's'. We will not hear another word spoken for more than ten minutes, as Scottie sees Madeleine and then embarks on the task and pleasure of silently tracking her. The two expository scenes, with their small-scale pattern of shot-by-shot alternation between characters, fit into a larger-scale pattern of alternation between blocks of dialogue and non-dialogue scenes – one can't say 'silent' because, in addition to the normal range of sound effects, Herrmann's music is so prominent. This structure is evident from the table in Figure 1, which covers the first 40 minutes of the film, from the end of the credits to the scene where Scottie and Madeleine make contact for the first time. (Timings are calculated at film speed, as opposed to the slightly faster TV speed, and are rounded off to the nearest five seconds.)

Figure 1	Length	Number of shots	POV shots	Talk or non-talk
Rooftop	1.35	25	4	NT
Scottie and Midge	6.20	62	1	T
Scottie and Elster	5.35	44	0	T
Ernie's	1.40	15	4	NT
Tracking Madeleine (1)	13.50	160	57	NT
Follow-up scenes	7.50	39	3	T
Tracking Madeleine (2)	2.50	32	10	NT

Total: Talk sections, 19 mins 55 seconds, 145 shots, including 8 POV (5.5%)
Non-talk sections, 19 mins 45 seconds, 232 shots, including 71 POV (30.6%)

Not all the categories are clear-cut – it is sometimes, as on the rooftop and in the restaurant, hard to decide whether certain shots technically represent POV, and lines of dialogue occur occasionally in passages marked as non-dialogue (and vice versa) – but the basic pattern is clear and striking. It will be apparent at once that the non-dialogue sections contain a large number of POV shots, and the dialogue sections almost none. The pattern of alternating modes is one that can be traced right back to one of the films on which Powell worked with Hitchcock, *Blackmail*, made in 1929, when the British industry was starting to convert to synchronised sound. Hitchcock shot it as a silent film, and then, when asked to add on some dialogue scenes, did so not in the form of a final talkie reel, but by spreading them evenly throughout the narrative, so that static passages of synchronised dialogue alternate with mobile, freely edited passages where we hear only music and a few sound effects; the most powerful of these convey the subjectivity of the oppressed heroine (Anny Ondra). *Blackmail* demonstrates systematically that – to adopt the terms Hitchcock used in the 1960s in the Truffaut interview – the tendency of the new technology to rely on 'photographs of people talking' can be offset by incorporating passages of authentic 'cinema'. Even though sound technology rapidly became more flexible, undermining the simplicity of the cinematic/theatrical opposition, Hitchcock continued to express an allegiance to non-dialogue aesthetics, insisting to Truffaut that 'the silent cinema was the purest form of cinema'.[48] Some of his later films return to the *Blackmail* pattern of studied alternation between different modes, *Rear Window*, *North by Northwest* and *Psycho* having particularly lengthy non-dialogue sections, but in none of them is the pattern as systematic as in *Vertigo*.

It is after the scene at Ernie's that the three-in-one mechanism of the cinematic look clicks into place, a narrative engine as smooth as that of the cars that the couple drive. Apart from a small number of shots that frame the two of them together in their cars, we will never, up to the time when she jumps into San Francisco Bay at the end of the second tracking sequence, see Madeleine except through Scottie's eyes: that is, through Hitchcock's camera, placed in the exact position which we have just been shown that Scottie occupies. Nor will we hear her speak.

The first tracking section covers four locations, within, it seems, the same day. Scottie waits for her in his car across the road from her apartment. When she sets off in her car he follows her: to flower shop, graveyard, art gallery and hotel. Losing her trail there, he returns to the apartment building and confirms that her car is back in place outside it. The most intense parts of this are based on pure alternation, i.e. a 50 per cent rate of POV shots. From his final gaze at the Elster couple as they leave the restaurant, we dissolve from his face to a daytime exterior:

1. Wide shot of Scottie's car waiting.
2. Closer shot, from side; Scottie at wheel, with newspaper; looks up

Pure alternation follows. In Figure 2, all the shots tabulated in the left-hand column show Scottie himself; all those on the right give us his POV, as he begins his observation of Madeleine. From shot 10, the shots of Scottie in his car are frontal ones. The tabulation brings out the extremely systematic nature of the alternation, which seals us firmly within Scottie's eyes and mind.

Figure 2	
	3 – scanning the high apartment block
4– at wheel, looks out:	5 – LS, she comes out, goes to car
6– at wheel	7 – her car pulls out
8– at wheel	9 – she goes past, he pulls out behind
10 – at wheel (frontal)	11 – car ahead, goes left
12 – at wheel	13 – car ahead, down hill
14 – at wheel	15 – car ahead, goes right
16 – at wheel	17 – car ahead, cuts across left
18 – at wheel, quizzical	19 – car turns into an alley
20 – at wheel, quizzical	21 – car drives down the alley
22 – at wheel: following	23 – car stops
24 – stops: peers	25 – Madeleine gets out, goes in door
– then a four-shot interlude as Scottie catches up:	
26 – opens car door	
27 – wider shot: exits car	
28 – walks to door	
29 – reaches door	
– and back to pure alternation:	
30 – (from inside): enters	31 – dark corridor with brooms etc.
32 – walks forward	33 – forward movement to door at end

34 – opens door, looks:	35 – Madeleine in flower shop, speaking to assistant

36 – a more complex shot: he shrinks back in the doorway as she walks about, visible to us in a mirror adjacent to him.

	37 – Madeleine waiting (as 35): receives posy

– and the pattern continues as they move on to the next stage of the ritual:

38 – closes door, back along corridor to outer door	
39 – exit, walk to car	
40 – (frontal) settles at wheel	41 – Madeleine exits to car (matches shot 25)
42 – at wheel	43 – car draws away …

It is the purest embodiment of Hitchcock's concept of 'pure cinema', based on the principle of systematic alternation that had been developed, though with little or no POV element, in D. W. Griffith's multitudinous short films for Biograph between 1908 and 1913, and refined and theorised by the Soviet film-makers whose influence, like that of Griffith, Hitchcock always acknowledged. In Pudovkin's terms, the car scenes are classic 'creative geography', constructing a continuity of cinematic time and space out of components made at different times and in different spaces: background plates, studio shots of James Stewart at the wheel, exteriors of Madeleine's Jaguar in traffic. When the components are put together, first in the process shots of him, and then in the editing, the scene flows hypnotically.

A similar pattern underlies the next sequence, in which he follows her to the Mission Dolores, and through the church to the small graveyard at the back. As he spots her among the gravestones, we return to pure alternation: ten shots of Scottie, moving about discreetly and peering at her, intercut with ten shots through his eyes. After her exit, Scottie moves forward to identify the headstone where she has lingered: it is that of Carlotta Valdes, 1831–1857. Catching her up, he follows her to the art gallery at the Palace of the Legion of Honor, some way out of the city centre. The rhythm continues, with another passage of alternation for the central section: five shots of Scottie, and five shots from his POV, as she sits contemplating a large female portrait. The long wordless passage is now interrupted by a brief exchange which Madeleine, seated deep in the background, is not privy to: in answer to

Hitchcock's 'pure cinema', based on alternation: the silent tracking begins

Scottie, the gallery attendant identifies the portrait as that of Carlotta, and gives him the catalogue for future reference.

Madeleine, under the direction of Hitchcock and, one stage back, Elster, has by now exhibited herself, with apparently innocent seductiveness, in three especially blatant and radiant poses, each time in profile: at Ernie's (to Scottie at the bar), at the flowershop (to Scottie hiding behind the door, shots 35–7 in Figure 2) and in the graveyard (to Scottie lurking among the stonework). This time, she 'exhibits' herself plus the portrait of Carlotta, and Scottie duly pieces together the connections.

Figure 3	
	1 – Madeleine, and the portrait she is gazing at
2 – Scottie (looks)	3 – from her posy to that in the picture
4 – Scottie (looks)	5 – from the hair to that in the picture
6 – Scottie (looks)	7 – portrait: face + necklace
8 – Scottie (looks)	9 – wider shot, as 1
10 – Scottie (moves away)	

Shots 3 and 5 give us the movement of Scottie's eyes and brain with the fierce directness of the subjective vertigo-effect shots. The camera moves up from the posy which Madeleine bought, and which she did not, as we might have expected, lay on the grave, to close in on the identical one held in the portrait; cut back to his face as he registers this (shot 4), then to the tight circular motif in Madeleine's hair, and up again to close in on

Madeleine in the gallery: shots 1 and 9 in Figure 3

Scottie looks at Carlotta's necklace: shots 6–7–8

Carlotta's identical style. This little sequence of alternation is enclosed within the two wider shots, 1 and 9, but what about shot 7? It spells out no third link between gazer and portrait, but simply frames, in a static shot, the upper body of Carlotta, the most prominent adornment of which is a necklace. Madeleine is not wearing one, nor is this the same necklace that she was wearing at Ernie's. There is a gap here waiting to be filled, or, if you like, Hitchcock and his writers are laying down a clue.

Now she leads him to the McKittrick Hotel, a nineteenth-century wooden building set back from the road. After seeing her enter, and look out of the first-floor front window – and then move away from it, so that he feels he can go in undetected – Scottie talks to the woman who runs it. She tells him that the young woman who rents the room, Carlotta Valdes, has not been in today; when they look, the room is indeed empty, nor is her car outside, nor has her key been taken from behind the reception desk. As Hitchcock and his collaborators saw it, the mystery of her disappearance would be a prime topic for 'icebox' discussion. Madeleine could have had another key on her, have slipped upstairs without being seen, and then have gone out by a back way; she could be the ghost of Carlotta, materialising and dematerialising herself at will; Scottie, in his growing obsession, could have fantasised her presence. Thinking back on it, we are likely to infer that Elster had bribed the owner to collude in the deception. This is certainly the official explanation, as spelled out in the intermediate script documentation, but, as with so much of the first part of the film, an uncanny element lingers on repeated viewings.

The shot of Madeleine at the window is the last one that we or Scottie get of her for a long time. Since her entry into the film at Ernie's, his and our attention has been fixated on her. Even when she disappears, Scottie continues to look for her; of the next 33 shots, seven give us his point of view, of spaces where she has been, or might have been. This long section ends with Scottie coming full circle to the apartment block, and seeing the car parked outside, with the posy reassuringly – cunningly – left on the dashboard.

At this point we all, as it were, come up for air. Scottie goes to Midge, then with her to Pop Leibel, expert on local history, at the Argosy bookshop, and then to Elster. The film reverts to the very talky mode, and to the corresponding type of visual structure, devoid of POV shots (except briefly when Scottie is alone in the car, after taking Midge home, and looks at the catalogue picture of Carlotta, juxtaposing it with his memory-image of Madeleine at Ernie's). The function of this block of scenes is threefold: to give out further information, to us and to Scottie, mainly about Carlotta; to lure Scottie further into Elster's plot; and to chart his growing alienation from Midge.

Pop Leibel, the expert on old San Francisco, is presumably on the level. No one to my knowledge has argued that he is, as the hotel woman may be, in league with Elster. So his tale of Carlotta is presumably accurate; Elster must have acquired his own knowledge of this same case, and located the gravestone. The words Pop uses to narrate the history of the victimisation of 'the sad Carlotta' by an unnamed mid-nineteenth-century magnate – 'They could do it in those days: they had the power and the freedom' – echo what Elster said to Scottie in their first meeting. 'The things that spell San Francisco to me are disappearing fast': what he regrets is the passing of 'colour, excitement, power, freedom'. And Elster is, of course, in the process of re-enacting that act of oppression, making victims both of his own wife and of Judy, whom he will ditch after the plot is completed. In its shadowy, atmospheric *mise-en-scène* as well as in dialogue, this scene summons up the old San Francisco in a more concentrated way than any other in the film, and suggests one of the functions of the Biercian rootedness noted earlier: *Vertigo* not only tells a story of male pride and oppression in its present day, but suggests that these attitudes have deep historical and cultural roots. As Pop Leibel says, in explaining about Carlotta, 'There are many such stories'.[49] While Midge responds to the story with a heartfelt 'poor thing!', Scottie sweeps straight out, and refuses boorishly to give away anything in response to her understandable curiosity as to what this is all about. He is already unbalanced by a romantic obsession, which Elster, in the next scene at his club, will skilfully feed.

From Elster's, as Scottie takes in the complexity of the Carlotta story, and of Madeleine's putative connection with it, a dissolve takes us again into the mode of wordless tracking: briefly, this time, to the art gallery, and then through the magnificent approaches to the Golden Gate Bridge. At Fort Point, at the edge of the bay, Madeleine deliberates, scatters the petals of her posy into the water, and then jumps in herself. Now Scottie can, at last, come out of hiding, and save her. Carrying her out of the water like a true romantic hero, he lays her comatose body down in her car, and speaks to her for the first time, husky from his immersion: 'Madeleine, Madeleine'. This is 28 minutes of story time since he first saw her and his obsession with her was born.

We now go to his apartment for the first time, having hitherto seen him only in public spaces and on other people's territory. This first direct meeting between them breaks down the pattern of the dialogue/non-dialogue alternation by involving her, at last, in conversation.

Scottie is putting wood on the fire, and an elaborate camera movement, right to left, measures out the space of his apartment in an echo of the first shot of Ernie's restaurant. This time, instead of drawing back and out from the expectant Scottie, it moves inward and round, and is thus tied more closely to his consciousness than its predecessor, less of a director's-eye view. Female clothes hanging up to dry in the kitchen area suggest what has happened since the scene at Fort Point, and the

Madeleine is apparently unconscious …

… and has now, it seems, been undressed and put to bed by Scottie

Scottie watches Madeleine in the cemetery

San Francisco then and now: the print on Elster's wall (1849), the city skyline (1957), the Mission Dolores …

… the Golden Gate Bridge, the redwood forest, the Palace of Fine Arts

Offering herself to the gaze. As Madeleine: at Ernie's, in the flower shop, in the mission graveyard …

… and at the Palace of the Legion of Honour. As Judy: outside the flower shop and in her hotel room after dinner at Ernie's

Scottie's gaze as the woman walks towards him: at Ernie's, after pulling her from the water, after the makeover is complete …

... and what he sees

Scottie looking on death: the policeman, Madeleine Elster, Judy Barton.

camera movement, as at Ernie's, comes to rest on the figure of Madeleine, in Scottie's bedroom, apparently sleeping off her ordeal. As, again, at Ernie's, the next shot is of Scottie, as he strains to make out the murmured words that come from the bed. The phone by the bed rings, Scottie answers it, Madeleine 'wakes', startled, and takes a bathrobe from him; he prepares coffee, then she joins him, speaking her first lines: 'What happened? Why am I here?'

The scene that follows, the pivotal one of the whole film, is extraordinary in its dramatic and emotional complexity, sustained by acting, scripting and direction of great delicacy. (The degree of commitment and teamwork that went into creating it is illustrated by the testimony of Art Director Henry Bumstead that he decided to give Scottie a hobby of stamp-collecting, and carefully put a variety of stamps and albums among the room's furnishings, earning Hitchcock's approval; I've never managed to see evidence of this on screen, but the lived-in quality of the décor may well have helped to deepen the performances).[50] At one level this seems like a tentative love scene of touching transparency. As Taylor wrote in his script directions, 'It is clear that they are very taken with one another.' Yet both of them are also caught up in complex layers of deceit, as if playing out in intense form a proof of the saying that there are six people involved in every encounter: the two people as they see themselves, the two as they are seen by the other, and the two as they really are, whatever that is. Even on a first viewing, the complex layers of this Scottie/Madeleine encounter are palpable, and when we know the plot they become dizzying.

Scottie sees Madeleine as a beautiful married woman haunted by the past. She knows that she is not Madeleine at all but Judy, a single woman hired to impersonate her for criminal purposes. Scottie sees himself as a private investigator who knows more than she does, and who is getting emotionally involved in his case, while she sees him as a victim who knows less than she does, and whom she must keep leading on. And who are they, the man and the woman, really? Between them there hovers the unspoken knowledge that Scottie has undressed her and put her to bed. He believes her, obviously, to have been unconscious, as we do first time round; what she can't tell him is that she was acting, and presumably conscious throughout. Scottie himself is (as he thinks) keeping his own secret from her: the fact that his presence at Fort Point was no accident, but that he has been commissioned to keep her under surveillance. And here he is, starting to establish an intimacy with a woman who is not just (as he thinks) married to another man, but whom he is looking after as a favour to the husband, so he is starting to, in terms of what he knows, betray a trust. When she says to him 'I'm married, you know', he can't make a reply, but simply looks guilty in a schoolboyish way, guilty that he is not admitting to her that he knew this already (not that it is true!), and guilty that he has adulterous thoughts.

In the 1989 reworking of his Hitchcock book, Wood analyses the first Midge/Scottie scene in detail, and makes much of the pattern of alternate and separate shots, as being expressive of the two characters' inability to get close, except in an asexual mother/child relationship; in the only five shots

'It is clear that they are very taken with one another'

that frame them together, Midge is in some way 'mothering' him.[51] It's a convincing piece of close analysis, except to the extent that it implies this separate and alternate pattern of scene-construction to be *ipso facto* expressive of distance. Montage, as Hitchcock learned at an early stage both from the Soviet theorists and from his own practice, operates in more varied ways: the cutting together of separate shots can be used to convey similarity as well as contrast, intimacy as well as distance, depending on context and on details of composition, rhythm, performance, and so on. The pivotal scene between Scottie and Madeleine is in fact just as fragmented as the first Midge/Scottie scene. It comprises 86 shots in all, and the 50 shots at its centre, as they talk for the first time (16 to 65 inclusive), are pure alternation, though in shot 50 his hand does enter 'her' shot as he passes a coffee cup. We get, at the same time, a sense of intimacy and possibility and of complex if-onlys in their relationship, and a reminder that they remain two separate and rather unfathomable people with their two quite separate agendas. Simply in technical terms, matching eyelines and rhythms as they shift about, constructing an always coherent space and feeling of co-presence from these separate bits of film, the scene is breathtakingly accomplished.[52]

What follows is just as delicate in its play with space, time and viewpoint. As their talk grows more intimate, Scottie offers to get her more coffee, and reaches for her cup; their hands touch, and we can see, within a two-shot, that for both of them this is a moment of erotic tension and possibility (see the still on the cover of this book). Immediately, the phone rings, the tension is broken, and Scottie leaves the room to answer it. When he returns, she has gone. Midge, driving past, observes her departure, followed by Scottie's baffled exit to look for her.

The call is, of course, from Elster, and its timing is uncannily precise, to the second, allowing them to get so far but no further. In retrospect and on repeat viewings, we realise that Elster is controlling events, but how does he know the exact moment at which to phone? It's as if his co-conspirator Madeleine has pressed a hidden button to alert him, or as if he has been monitoring the scene via closed-circuit cameras. If he is the remote-control director of events, then the on-set director is Hitchcock, and there is nothing uncanny about *his* choosing the exact moment, as scripted, for the bell to ring. The scene between the two began with Elster's first phone call, like a cue to Madeleine for 'action', and the phone call that ends it is like the call of 'cut', or perhaps more accurately 'wrap for the day', after which she is free to go home.

Madeleine appeared to be asleep before the first call, and to be woken by it, though we learn later that she was only pretending to sleep – which of course would have been true of the actress, Kim Novak, within either of the two scenarios. Behind Elster, then, we can sense the other string-puller, Hitchcock, choosing the dramatically most tense and telling moment for the scene to start and end. For Scottie, innocent of the plot, the timing is indeed devastating, like an alarm bell from his conscience, reminding him of his obligation to the anxious husband, or from his superego, holding him back from pursuing his desire.

As he exits from the frame, the camera holds Madeleine for a moment as her eyes follow him: the very first time we have seen her in her own right, as it were, independently of Scottie. The next shot shows us, briefly, what she sees, Scottie going through the door into his study, but the POV shot is not confirmed, in Hitchcock's normal manner, by going back to the shot of her looking – our access to her is still only fleeting. Cut instead to Scottie picking up the phone. The conversation is sustained, by Elster and by Hitchcock, for long enough to give Madeleine 'time' to get dressed in her own clothes and leave – not literally, since she is heard departing after only 40 seconds, but cinematically it *seems* long enough. Scottie puts down the phone and goes to look: both she and the hung-up clothes have gone: his POV shot is, unlike hers, bracketed on either side by shots of his face, returning us to the familiar alignment with his viewpoint. But when he goes back towards the phone, we cut not to the completion of the conversation with Elster, but to Madeleine's exit, and to a third viewpoint, that of Midge, who just happens – though for all we know she may do it regularly – to be driving down the steep hill outside Scottie's house at the moment Madeleine leaves. In Figure 4, all the shots in the right column are identical camera set-ups, showing the apartment exterior from a point across the street from the house and somewhat above; the shots on the left are all of Midge:

Figure 4	
	1 – Madeleine exit
2 – Midge drives down steep street	
3 – (closer) brakes; looks	4 – Midge's POV: Madeleine drives off
5 – (to herself): 'was it a ghost, was it fun?'	6 – Midge's POV: Scottie comes out onto the porch
7 – drives off out of shot	8 – Scottie looking

Shot 1 is Hitchcock's 'objective' camera position; Midge then inserts herself into it, inhabits it for two shots, and then relinquishes it. For a moment, this seems to align, literally, the director, and the spectator, with her viewpoint, that of everyday normality. But Scottie and Madeleine go their own ways oblivious of her and what she represents, and we go with them.

Scottie waits again the next day outside Madeleine's apartment block, and is relieved to see Madeleine emerge. The film slips back smoothly into its mode of sustained silent tracking, sealing us anew within Scottie's eyes and mind, as his car takes up position behind her and follows it, to his increasing puzzlement, back to his own place. She has come to deliver a letter of thanks and apology and – in plot terms – to keep him hooked, if that were needed. They agree that they should now wander together, rather than separately.

Now that they are talking; now that she can look at him, and return his gaze, rather than simply offering herself to it in long shot or in profile; now that he has undressed her, and that they are both exquisitely conscious that the other knows this but can't refer to it; now that the Elster plot is starting to become very real and its consummation to draw near ... in these circumstances, Madeleine starts to look and act increasingly uneasy. The unease is, of course, for the most part absolutely 'in character' for a woman struggling against ghosts or demons. But as Scottie goes back to shut his door before getting into her car for their first drive together, the camera lingers for a second time, and for longer, on Kim Novak alone, out of his gaze, and we get an acute sense, if we know the plot, of the woman's anxiety at what she is getting herself into. This double quality is taken up in the two intense scenes that follow: the visits to the redwood park and to Cypress Point. She has a script to follow, and she does so assiduously, starting to feed out information about the dream that will soon lure Scottie down to the chosen murder spot; and again, the more troubled she becomes at going through with it, the better her behaviour suits the 'mad Carlotta' identity. The ancient trees that dwarf them, and the even more ancient ocean that explodes into spray behind their kiss, are highly appropriate props and backdrops both for her haunted-by-the-past act and for the romantic scenario that she needs to keep encouraging; but they seem to impress and move her as much as they do Scottie, and the spectator.

At this point we return to Midge. After the bookstore visit, she told Scottie she was going to take a look for herself at the Carlotta portrait.

Scottie and Madeleine kiss at Cypress Point

Since then, she has observed Madeleine's exit from his house. She was established at the start as an artist, and, when Scottie now calls in with a low-key visit to the movies in mind, she unveils her own reworking of the portrait: in it, she herself occupies Carlotta's place, incongruously wearing her own sensible spectacles above Carlotta's necklace. The effect, predictably, is to alienate Scottie even further. Rather than going out with her, he walks back alone through Union Square, and seems to doze through the night on his couch, since he is there when, early next morning, Madeleine rings the doorbell.

Again, she feeds him lines from the Elster script, telling him more about the dreams that haunt her. The details lead him, as intended, to identify the location as the Mission of San Juan Bautista; they duly drive there, and Madeleine manoeuvres him into chasing her, vainly, up the belltower. Paralysed by his acrophobia, he can only watch through a window in horror as the woman's body falls from the top, to lie, plainly dead, on the tiles below him. Through these last scenes in the Madeleine persona, Kim Novak takes to even intenser levels the doubleness of her role – in-character disturbance, and genuine turmoil – until for the first time she utters a line that hardly makes sense within the Elster script: 'It wasn't supposed to happen this way, it shouldn't have happened.' But by now she is close to the tower and to the agreed moment, and she gives Scottie no chance to interrogate her further. 'Let me go to the church, alone.' To his anguished question why, she gives him the most effective substitute for an answer: having already insisted that she loves him, she immobilises him for just long enough with a final kiss.

As she runs away from him, and he realises where she is heading, he repeats the first words he spoke to her after pulling her from the water: 'Madeleine, Madeleine'. But this time she is not in his grasp, nor can he save her. The shock of his inability to do so literally strikes him dumb.

The protracted silence of Madeleine in the first section of the film is balanced by the protracted silence of Scottie that follows her exit. In trailing her, he was necessarily silent himself, but those periods of voyeuristic absorption were active, and broken up by dialogue scenes. Now, he is passive. Looking helplessly at the dead body below him, he registers trauma by the gesture of slowly covering his mouth with his right hand, then slinks away to avoid confrontation. (Any such post-mortem confrontation would, of course, have threatened the Elster plot, since Scottie might very well then have seen whose body it actually was; the fact that both Elster and Hitchcock here 'get away with it' indicates how powerfully both Scottie and audience are being controlled, and how boldly the film is defining its own terms for plausibility – poetic and psychological rather than literal). At the inquest, Scottie writhes silently under the protracted verbal barbs of the coroner, and the looks of those around him; afterwards, he remains silent through one-sided conversations with an ostensibly sympathetic Elster and with the police officer in whose care he departs. His silent visit to Madeleine's grave is followed by his nightmare, from which he wakes without even the release of a scream. Next, he is in hospital, a broken man, giving a blank response to Midge's despairingly persistent conversational gambits; if Madeleine began as passive object of the gaze, Scottie has become passive object of the voice. It took 28 minutes of screen time, after her first entrance, for Madeleine to speak; here, Scottie is silent for 14 minutes, during most of which he is present on screen. Meanwhile, his visual sense too has atrophied. After the traumatising POV shots of the falling and then prone body, we get no more shots of this kind, other than a few low-key POV images, from his static position, of the male faces around him at the inquest. His visit to Madeleine's grave is not marked by the POV shot we would normally expect of the stone and its inscription, but is taken in a single listless wide shot. The nightmare is by definition subjective, an eruption of memory and anxiety; waking, he shuts himself down. At the hospital he looks blankly into space, and in his scene there with Midge the only POV shots, as well as the only words, belong to her. Blank passivity is, of course, only what we would expect in a film that depicts a mental breakdown; the distinction of *Vertigo* is, through scripting, direction and acting, to enact it with such graphic precision in terms of both image and sound, and to place it within such a precise and compelling overall architecture.

A strong break follows, like a division between acts. Midge talks with a doctor about Scottie's fixation on the dead woman, in the first scene from which he has been absent; she then walks slowly down the hospital corridor, away from the camera and out of the film.

'You don't even know I'm here'

Midge walks away

REVELATION
. . . .

A slow fade-out is followed by a re-establishing pan over a long shot of the city and the bay. Several months have passed. Now released from hospital, Scottie has resumed his mourning of Madeleine in the manner of Thomas Hardy's mourning of his wife, as described in the extraordinarily intense series of *Poems of 1912–1913* that includes 'After a Journey':

> Hereto I come to view a voiceless ghost ...
> Yes, I have re-entered your olden haunts at last;
> Through the years, through the dead scenes, I have tracked you.

Scottie returns to the olden haunts of, successively, the apartment block, Ernie's and the art gallery at the Palace of the Legion of Honor; each time, *mise en scène* and camera placement recreate the 'dead scenes' of the first part, and the voiceless ghost of Madeleine seems for a moment to materialise before solidifying into a more mundane form. The fourth location is the flower shop, seen from an unfamiliar streetfront angle, but displaying a posy like the one Madeleine bought there, and it is while he is lingering by it that he sees a young woman, at the end of the working day, chatting with friends in the street. Neither ethereal nor elegant, she has just enough of a look of Madeleine to interest him, and the resemblance reanimates his rusty skills in visual tracking, triggering a return to the mode of silent alternation, over a 20-shot sequence, between shots of him and shots from his POV, as he follows her through the streets to her hotel; there is even an echo, as she opens the window of her upstairs room, of his view of Madeleine at the McKittrick Hotel. Likewise, when he enters and knocks at her door, he starts, falteringly, to rediscover the power of fluent speech – we have only, in the preceding scenes, heard him speak a few strained words.

The scene that develops in her room has obvious parallels with the long scene in Scottie's apartment that followed the leap into the bay: a meeting in bizarre circumstances, a getting-acquainted conversation, a strong reciprocal interest, overlaid by complex layers of inhibition and deception. Even though neither of them is any longer playing out a masquerade at Elster's bidding, they are still operating in his shadow – and, of course, under the unrelenting control of his director double.

Scottie has no cause to doubt the woman's identification of herself as Judy Barton from Kansas, who works in a store, and who simply reminds him of the Madeleine he loved and lost. When she ends her account of herself and her background with the word 'honest', and a shy, open, touching smile, it seems that she is, in these respects, *being* honest, and that Scottie is getting an accurate picture of the young woman who was picked up previously by Elster, exploited for her resemblance to his wife, and then returned abruptly to her previous station. His response to her is likewise honest, oppressively curious but also diffident. He even repeats what he did in the two initial scenes with Midge and then Elster, going to the door as if to exit, then turning back to allow himself to be drawn in further: he invites her to dinner, and she accepts.

. . . .

I have experimented with a video re-editing of *Vertigo*, to eliminate the confession scene that follows, so that we go directly from Scottie's exit to his first date with Judy, at Ernie's. This simply restores the structure that was firmly in place up to the final script revision, and that Hitchcock tried hard to get back to at the last minute by asking for all prints to be called back for alteration. But it's impossible, of course, to form an authentic and judicious response to this version when one is already familiar with the film as released; one would need to monitor the reactions of a first-time audience, and I'm not sure if one has the moral, let alone contractual, right to set up such an exercise now, messing around with people's first experience of the film. The original feedback from previews of the shorter version evidently discouraged Paramount from agreeing to the last-minute excision.[53]

Even with the confession scene cut, and even on a first screening, we are likely to be more suspicious than Scottie of the Madeleine lookalike; trailer and publicity have confirmed that this is again Kim Novak, and we expect a further plot-twist before the end. The wearing of Carlotta's necklace then becomes the big clue, for us as it is for Scottie, and we struggle to piece together, alongside him, the truth, and to take in the reconstruction of it to which she finally, halfway up the tower, assents. We may or may not have anticipated it, just as we may or may not, on a first viewing of *Psycho*, have anticipated the identity of the murderous Mrs Bates before the moment when the wig falls off. But that moment of identification is visual, the build-up to it has been deliberately paced, and the scene that follows with the psychiatrist enables us to reflect. The end of *Vertigo* is much more compressed and abrupt, and becomes even more so in the alternate 'end-heavy' version.

How much difference would this make on repeated viewings? We adjust to the loss of the surprise factor on repeat viewings of *Psycho*; we in any case, on repeat viewings of *Vertigo*, look in a new way, and with deeper fascination, at all of Judy's pre-confession scenes, first as Madeleine and then as herself; we could surely do the same with the shorter section that follows. What difference does it make to have the official revelation postponed a bit further? It is, all the same, hard to imagine *Vertigo* exerting quite the hold it does, and enjoying the status it does, in that shorter version. Not only would the constructional

Judy explaining her background – 'honest' ...

... and revealing her dark secrets to us, though not to Scottie

imbalance be felt as a continuing flaw, but the confession scene adds material for which later information is no substitute. The quick visual précis of exactly what happened at the top of the tower between Elster and the two Madeleines is indispensable, and so is our one scene of unmediated access to Judy.

At no other point in the film do we see her, in either persona, independently of Scottie. Either he is trailing her, in which case we see her solely through his eyes, or he is with her; the one technical exception to this is the rapid four-shot montage of refashioning – eyes, mouth, hair, nails – to which, as Judy, she will submit at his brutal insistence. In contrast to the flow of Scottie's subjective images, we get scarcely any images from her POV. At the end of the first long silent part of her masquerade, as she waits, under Scottie's intent gaze, to jump into the bay, she scatters petals into the water, and we look down at them with her. At the end of the first long conversation in Scottie's apartment, we see though her eyes as Scottie goes out of the room to answer Elster's phone call. In the redwood forest, two shots seem to represent a shared POV, as she and Scottie look together at the cross-section of the tree with its historical dating, and she makes explicit her supposed identity with the dead Carlotta. Then, in the course of the drive south to the mission, we see her POV of the road in front, and the trees above. These few, mainly unobtrusive shots give us fleeting access to her viewpoint at a series of climactic moments in the process of her exploitation by Elster, and of their joint exploitation of Scottie, and they acquire extra poignancy in retrospect, as glimpses of a subjective experience that we recognise as being as complex and as emotional as Scottie's.

As Judy Barton, she has, likewise, been seen by us only as Scottie sees her: first through his POV images, then in conversation with him. As he exits, saying he will pick her up for dinner in an hour, we stay with her, and she turns slowly to face the camera. Dissolve to the visual précis of what happened on the tower, culminating in the fall of the body. She prepares to pack her bags, then writes Scottie a letter whose text we hear in voice-over. She confesses what happened – 'You were the victim, I was the tool.' Loving him, she has longed for this meeting, and also dreaded it because of the need, if she is to get to know him afresh, to keep lying, the dangers of which she now can't face. It can be inferred that, like the ghost of Hardy's wife, she herself has been revisiting the 'dead scenes', and that it is no accident that she has paused in front of one of those scenes, the flower shop with the posy in its window, to display her right profile 'innocently' to the observing Scottie, just as she did in her earlier persona at Ernie's, at the flower shop and in the mission garden.

The letter ploy is, like so much in the film, hardly plausible in realistic terms. She will have a rush to pack and leave before he returns to pick her up; even if she succeeds, she would expect him, and/or the police, once the letter is read, to catch up with her, and to pursue Elster. We can see the letter both as a narrational device, and as a psychological release for her; before finishing it, she does what we have just seen Scottie do for the third time, namely reverse a decision to walk away, drawn by a compulsion similar to his to continue in the bolder, riskier course.

A dissolve takes us once more to Ernie's restaurant, as they embark on the relationship that we know represents, for both, their deepest desire, yet they don't look as if this is so. They are eating in silence, and it is the silence less of absorbed lovers than of uncommunicative distance. Scottie is still conditioned to go on looking for the phantom Madeleine, who seems, once again, momentarily to materialise in answer to his will; and we see that Judy perceives what is in his mind. The closest parallel I can think of for the heightened poignancy and irony of this situation is the last section of the great romantic melodrama *Random Harvest*, directed by Mervyn Le Roy for MGM in 1942, in which the amnesiac Ronald Colman longs to recapture the half-remembered intensity of his love for his lost first wife (Greer Garson), not knowing, as we do, that the second wife on whose loving support he relies is the same woman. It is crucial in psychological terms – and in generic terms, which really amounts to the

Back at Ernie's: Scottie looks away …

… and Judy too sees the false Madeleine

same thing – that the woman cannot in these situations make the obvious announcement that 'You don't need to keep looking, it's me'; her task, and that of the film, is to bring the man, somehow, to the point of active enlightenment, recognition and re-awakened love. *Vertigo*, of course, gives an agonising extra twist to this through the woman's dread of recognition, battling with her desire for it. As the shooting script puts it, when Scottie looks away from their table towards the Madeleine lookalike: 'Judy is staring at him anxiously. It is her first defeat, and her first victory: defeat, in that although he is with her he is still searching; victory, in that she is sure, now, that he does not think she is Madeleine.'

It is, then, like a stalemate, and the scene in her apartment when he drops her off spells this out. He wants to take care of her, disclaiming any sexual motives: 'I just want to be with you, to see you as much as I can.' 'Because I remind you of someone? That's not very complimentary. And nothing would … happen?' 'No'. 'That's not very complimentary either.' But if she wants him somehow to get to the point of reciprocating her love and desire, her only chance is to stay around him. The next two scenes re-enact the stalemate. They walk together by the Palace of Fine Arts, and this time it is she who looks yearningly away, at a young couple embracing on the grass, while Scottie walks staidly on, oblivious of them and, it seems, of her. Next they are shuffling together on a dance floor in a sedate and middle-aged ambience; this is the sedate, middle-aged Scottie of the film's early scenes. He might almost be with Midge, and Judy's inability to reach him is reminiscent of Midge's. Just as his companionate friendship with Midge contrasted with a memory of desire located back in 'the good old college days', so his companionship with Judy contrasts with his continuing obsession with Madeleine. Midge is still Midge, but has moved, it seems, irrecoverably beyond that youthful self; Judy has *been* Madeleine, vividly and recently.

The only way to break the stalemate is to risk being Madeleine again, which explains why she goes along with Scottie's decision to make her over. His decision to do so is introduced with brutal suddenness, and brutally carried out. Buying a buttonhole for her in the street, he simply announces that he will now buy her new clothes, and sets about it relentlessly and imperiously, overriding her clear distress. The clothes are Madeleine's: the same black gown she wore the first time at Ernie's, and the same grey suit that she wore the rest of the time, the original of which we know she still has in her hotel closet. As Madeleine, she was palpably torn, in the later stages of the Elster plot, between two kinds of distress, acted and real, and so she is here, except that both kinds of distress now seem equally real: the natural distress, as perceived by Scottie and the saleswoman, of one being treated so roughly, and the fear of exposure.

The next scene, in the apartment which she can't reveal that she has, as Madeleine, visited twice before, is equally intense and painful, showing them in the grip of a process that puzzles and frightens them both, but that they can't stop:

JUDY: Why are you doing this? What good'll it do?
SCOTTIE: I don't know, I don't know, no good I guess, I don't know ....
JUDY: I remind you of her, and not even that very much.
SCOTTIE: No, no, Judy, it's you too, there's something in you that ....
JUDY: Couldn't you like me, just the way I am? .... Well, I'll wear the darn clothes if you want me to, if you'll just, just like me. (*but he is distracted, staring at her face*)
SCOTTIE: The colour of your hair ....
JUDY: Oh no ....
SCOTTIE: Judy, please, it can't matter to you.
JUDY: If I let you change me, will it do it, if I do what you tell me, will you love me?
SCOTTIE: Yes, yes.
JUDY: All right, then I'll do it.

Since Scottie saw Judy in the street, we have been led to empathise fairly equally with them. We are alongside Scottie in following and meeting her, then stay with her for the confession scene; for the next six scenes they are together, and his POV shot in Ernie's, looking over her shoulder for the phantom Madeleine, is matched by hers of the lovers by the lake. If anything we are more inward with her; her understanding of what he looks away at is not reciprocated. Now, the focus shifts back decisively to Scottie. As he tells the beautician exactly what he wants, she is already off screen, and all we will see of this final makeover is the set of four clinically fragmented close-ups. Meanwhile, Scottie is back at her hotel room, and we stay in suspense with him, waiting and watching, until she returns; and after she agrees to make the one final change, by putting her hair up, we wait with him again.

The scene that follows is one of those that was already scripted in vivid outline a year ahead of shooting, after the first set of conferences between Hitchcock and Alec Coppel – it was one of the big moments that Hitchcock habitually, it seems, visualised at an early stage of considering a story, and around which a fully worked-out structure, with the help of his writers, then gradually cohered. The final version is heightened still further: by extending the suspense, with the camera holding Scottie without a cut for nearly a minute as he waits for the final unveiling of Judy-as-Madeleine; by lighting effects, which suffuse Scottie with a green glow from the neon sign outside the hotel, and place a diffusion filter in front of Madeleine as she first reappears to him; by the superimposing on the couple, as they kiss, of the livery stable at the mission where they kissed shortly before the fall from the tower; and by Herrmann's music, underscoring first the suspense and then the passion. Scottie's dream has become real, as has Judy's; the stalemate is over.

The next scene is one of post-coital contentment. Judy is wearing the black dress evening dress without protest, relaxing into her role not exactly *as* Madeleine, but as a Judy who is ready to make her man happy by being like Madeleine; as a woman from a modest background ready now to 'blossom' in response to true love, and to a milieu of greater sophistication. At least, that is how one guesses she would play it. There is no time to find out. As soon as they find happiness, they lose it.

Helping her to fasten her necklace, Scottie gets a good view of it in the mirror, and at once recognises it as the distinctive one worn in the portrait by Carlotta. A lot of careful planning was invested in this plot device; at one stage the script even had Scottie exploring the possibility that the necklace might be a duplicate, or have been bought second-hand. As it is, we know him to be much more familiar with it than Judy realises him to be. All she knows is that he will have seen it on Carlotta in the portrait, when she, as Madeleine, sat in front of it. Even then, she was successfully drawing his attention to the hair and the posy, by copying them; she did not wear the necklace too, and Scottie's eyes were thus not so consciously drawn to it. But we know, as she does not, that he has seen it again in the catalogue (via his memory-image of it, after the visit to Pop Leibel), and again in the reworking of the portrait by Midge, and again in his nightmare, when the camera actually moved in on the Carlotta portrait to centre it, as if by delayed action. We have also heard Elster tell Scottie that Carlotta's jewellery was handed down in the family. In terms of the 'yarn', then, it is made as plausible as it could be for her to be careless, for him to be alert, and for her to be slow to catch on to what he has realised, and to what he is doing in response.

He does not question or challenge her straight off, but drives south to the mission. They are locked, once again, into a regime of mutual deception, but of a more oppressive kind than at any time before. Two shots from her POV, of the road in front and the trees above, convey in the most direct way possible, since they are almost identical with those used earlier, her sense of being trapped in the compulsive replaying of a male-driven scenario; but though she must suspect, from the direction of the drive and from Scottie's changed manner, that he has guessed the truth, he gives nothing away – not enough for her to risk meeting him halfway and confessing on her own account, as she did in the torn-up letter. For his part, Scottie seems positively to relish the concealment. Not until he has driven the full distance (and the mission is nearly 100 miles from the city), and dragged her almost up to the 'scene of the crime' at the top of the tower, does he bring out his trump card, his recognition of the necklace, and lay out, triumphantly, the full scenario that he has now reconstructed from it.

His saved-up savagery is explained by the savagery of his pain; her anguish re-enacts the anguish she felt the first time they were there. She insists that they can still love each other, and persuades him into a brief embrace, passionate like their embrace at the stables a year ago, and like the embrace in the room that has just conjured up the stables in memory. But the first time, she looked away, over his shoulder – to the obligation that was calling her, in the shape of Elster, and of his wife's body. And now she looks away again, in a similar close-up: what she sees, a black figure coming up the steps, causes her to start back, and a scream tells us and Scottie that she has fallen. Cut back, for the film's final shot, to the black figure of the nun who has come up the steps because she 'heard voices', and who now crosses herself and rings the bell. The camera pulls back to a position outside the tower, framing Scottie as he comes forward to the edge, arms spread out, looking down to where the body has fallen.

A further scene was scripted, shot and included in some of the early

At the mission the first time – breaking off at the demands of the Elster plot

The second time – breaking off at the sight of the nun

prints. Scottie returns to Midge's apartment to look dumbly out of the window, with a large drink, while the radio gives news of Gavin Elster's arrest in Switzerland. The scene was evidently part of the film as shown in at least one country, Finland, and it was also there in the film as previewed in England, before being removed in time for the press show.[54] The obvious explanation for the scene is insurance against the possibility that censors in some countries might require the bringing to justice of the criminal to be made explicit. However, it has other, structural, functions, and Hitchcock's cutting notes show that it was only at a late stage that he decided to drop it from his preferred final version; without it, the ending is daring in its abruptness. In the shooting script:

> Scottie swings around again, steps quickly to the edge and looks down. He backs away, his face tight with horror, and holds the stonework for support. The nun comes into the shot. She steels herself to look below. She crosses herself.
>
> THE NUN
> God have mercy ...
>
> She reaches out for the bell cord.
>
> INT. THE BELL TOWER – (NIGHT)
>
> The church bell is tolling. It swings in and out of the picture. Through the archway we can see the mission garden below. Figures are hurrying across towards the church.
>
> DISSOLVE TO:
>
> INT. MIDGE'S APARTMENT – (NIGHT)

The dropping of the final scene is thus not the only change. The film abandons any glimpses of everyday even-keel reality (of the kind that the end of *Psycho* will return us to): the hurrying figures below, as well as the city, the radio and Midge.

This is consistent with the hermetic intensity of the final 40 minutes. Since Midge walked down the corridor after her talk with the doctor, the film has effectively been a two-hander: the two stars, and some single-scene bit-players. The only characters who speak at all, and then only briefly, are the Jaguar-owner, two shop staff, the nun, and a single male, the flower-seller. While the first section moved between Scottie's silent tracking of Madeleine and talk with others (Midge, Elster, Pop Leibel), and drove on in the exploration of a mystery, the last section has alternated silent scenes with talk between the couple alone. There is no release of tension, no 'coming up for air', and no mystery to explore, other than how the stalemate will be resolved. The film becomes an extraordinarily intense psychodrama, taking us deep into the pair's extreme emotions, Scottie's especially.

The last section, in effect, has fused two kinds of narrative. On the one hand, the romantic narrative, the drive to recapture the lost love. On the other, the paranoid narrative, the drive to unravel the conspiracy. Both come to a resolution of maximum intensity: as in the *Random Harvest* model the woman *is* rediscovered, as in classic film noir the conspiracy *is* unravelled, and the woman's guilt exposed. They are at the same time interdependent and incompatible: the dream can't be fully recaptured unless she is the same woman, but that involves explaining how she can be, which destroys the dream. Since we already know the truth, the experience of the final section is like watching two trains speeding inexorably towards each other on the same track – and being carried on both of them, along with the two characters.

What if Scottie had been content to accept the reality of Judy, opening himself to the possibility of loving her (in the words of the torn-up letter) 'as I am, for myself', or (in the words of her later plea to him) 'just me, the way I am', without the compulsion to make her over? What if she had not put the necklace on, at the moment when, for the first time, they are relaxed and happy together? What if the nun had not appeared, at the moment when, for the very first time, they are being completely open and honest with each other? All such questions, pertinent as they are, are swept aside in the acceleration towards the final crash.

Who is to blame? Most critics are hard on Scottie, for being, as Truffaut put it, a 'maniac'. He is indeed frightening both in his insistence on making Judy over ('it can't matter to you'), and, after the necklace scene, in his controlled and sustained vindictiveness. But, to state the obvious, he has a lot to be vindictive about, in view of what he has discovered about the plot in which he was both tool and victim, and in which Judy was an accomplice. The shadow of Elster hangs over it all: the donor of the necklace, the framer of Scottie, the seducer of Judy, the master-criminal of the tower whom Judy may even at first imagine is coming up the stairs at the end, and about whose arrest and extradition we hear in the deleted epilogue.

But how real is Elster? Perhaps the ultimate key to *Vertigo*'s fascination is the consummate way in which, from the start, it fuses two modes of narrative, which can loosely be called objective and subjective. We can glance back here to that other story that begins with a fall and a miraculous-seeming survival, *A Matter of Life and Death*. A written title introduces it as, explicitly, a story of two worlds, one 'real' and the other 'in the mind of' the faller, the David Niven character. Despite this, and despite the visual markers of difference between the worlds, publicity was still able to play on the film's uncanny dimension with the line 'Was it a Dream or Did it Really Happen?' The same question is pertinent to *Vertigo*, in which there is no *division* between worlds, but rather a hesitation. On the one hand, it is a carefully crafted 'yarn', the story of the character, Scottie, of what happens to him, and of how he responds, located in a detailed and recognisable California environment. On the other, it is famously dreamlike both in its texture and in the way it introduces story and protagonist. Echoing Robin Wood, James Maxfield argues that 'everything after the opening sequence is ... dream or fantasy', and both of them on this basis develop comprehensive accounts of Scottie's psychological journey.[55] If the film is his dream or fantasy, then the whole Elster plot naturally becomes his own construction rather than something imposed upon him. The opposition between the remote romantic female image (Madeleine) and the more earthy and available one (Judy) becomes part of his own scenario, expressive of a classic madonna/whore dichotomy. Each time he gets close to reconciling the two figures, and relating genuinely to the 'real' woman, he finds himself compelled to relinquish her immediately: hence the phone call, the necklace, the figure of the nun.

There are, as I have stressed, many Hitchcock films – and many non-Hitchcock ones – which have this double dimension; which tell stories in a perfectly straightforward and accessible manner, and at the same time operate *as if* playing out the inner desires and conflicts of their protagonist. But the women of *The Lady Vanishes* and *Suspicion*, and the men of *The 39 Steps* and *North by Northwest* (as indeed of *A Matter of Life and Death*), work through their anxieties in a productive and therapeutic way; there is no real clash between the two levels, and the resolution is positive. Of the films on this model, *Vertigo* has the strongest discordance between levels, and the most painful resolution, or lack of it. Another way of putting this is to say that it does not follow the classic route to the construction of the happy heterosexual couple, but problematises it radically. At the end, Scottie has overcome his vertigo successfully, representing one kind of reassertion of his masculine power, but has lost the woman. In Robin Wood's words, 'triumph and tragedy are indistinguishably fused'.[56]

But that is the final line of Wood's 1965 analysis, relatively sympathetic to Scottie and his romantic yearning, in which he writes that: 'Madeleine ... represents wish-fulfilment on a deeper and more valid level than that normally offered by the Hollywood film: by this point in the film [her apparent suicide] she has evoked in us all that longing for something beyond a daily reality which is so basic to human nature.'[57] His analysis in the 1989 chapter is critical both of that romanticism, and of Scottie's:

> The most obvious manifestation of this regression [to the infantile state] is the phenomenon called 'romantic love', with its demand for perfect union and its tendency to construct the loved person as an idealised fantasy figure: the necessary condition for the 'perfect union' being the denial of otherness and autonomy. It is this regression that *Vertigo* so incomparably dramatises: I know of no other film that so ruthlessly analyses the basis of male desire and exposes its mechanisms.[58]

This change of angle measures out a change, over the decades, in the values and priorities not only of Wood himself, but of Hitchcock studies, and of film studies. And yet the later passage doesn't exactly cancel out the first one. If 'all that longing' were not felt by the audience, as by Scottie, the film would not exert the power that it does. Likewise, however much we may want to pursue the *as-if* reading of the film, as a rigorous playing out of the hang-ups of this everyman of his time and place, we can only get access to them by submitting ourselves to the logic of the yarn, to the figure of Elster, and to the visual pleasure that he, and Hitchcock, lay out before Scottie, and us.

The French film-maker Chris Marker, one of the most acute of the commentators on *Vertigo*, has drawn attention to its artful pattern of ellipses: between Scottie's first sight of Madeleine and his trailing of her, eliding the decision; between his rescue of her from the bay and her waking in his bed, eliding his undressing of her; between their embrace in the hotel room and their preparation for dinner, eliding the love scene.[59] To these one can add the obvious one at the start, the ellipsis between Scottie hanging from the gutter and the first scene with Midge, and also a final one. What happens *after* the shot of Scottie looking down from the tower, as the nun rings the bell? If the epilogue is put back in, then an ellipsis here simply allows him to get down and back to Midge's apartment. But we can discount that; Sam Taylor himself forgot he had even written it, and suggested that Scottie had another breakdown, this time irreversible.[60] Others have suggested that he jumps off. But perhaps,

The end …

… looping back to the beginning … ?

instead, after this brief and unavailing mastery over it, his acrophobia returns. The film could complete the process of looping back to the beginning, in the manner of the classic Ealing horror film, *Dead of Night*, which likewise hesitates throughout between the modes of yarn and dream, and whose final shots repeat the initial ones, signalling that the story is about to replay itself. Scottie stumbles, and clings on, and is suddenly back in the city, suspended over the abyss, ready to go through it all again. After all, this is what so many of us are ready to do, time after time, alongside him.

NOTES

. . . .

1 Edward Buscombe, *Stagecoach* (London: BFI, 1992), p. 9.

2 Laura Mulvey, 'Visual Pleasure and Narrative Cinema', first published in *Screen*, Autumn 1975, reprinted in Mulvey, *Visual and Other Pleasures* (London: Macmillan, 1989), pp. 14–26.

3 Donald Spoto, *The Art of Alfred Hitchcock* (1976; London: W. H. Allen, 1977), p. 291.

4 Geoffrey O'Brien, 'Hitchcock's Masterpiece', in *The New York Review of Books*, 19 December 1996, p. 54.

5 Lynda Myles and Michael Goodwin, 'Alfred Hitchcock's San Francisco', in *San Francisco Magazine*, July 1982, pp. 50–7.

6 *Sight and Sound*, new series, vol. 2 no. 8, December 1992. Even in the 1982 poll, *Vertigo* had been ranked ninth.

7 Robert Kapsis, *Hitchcock: The Making of a Reputation* (Chicago: University of Chicago, 1992), p. 53.

8 C. A. Lejeune, reviews in *The Observer*, 7 August 1960 (*Psycho*) and 10 April 1960 (*Peeping Tom*).

9 Eric Rohmer and Claude Chabrol, *Hitchcock: The First Forty-Four Films* (New York: Ungar, 1979), p. 152. Original French publication as *Hitchcock* (Paris: Universitaires, 1957).

10 Richard Roud, 'The French Line', in *Sight and Sound*, vol. 29 no. 4, Autumn 1960, pp. 166ff.

11 Michael Powell, *A Life in Movies* (London: Heinemann, 1986), p. 520.

12 Robin Wood, *Hitchcock's Films* (London: Tantivy Press, 1965); reprinted as part of *Hitchcock's Films Revisited* (New York: Columbia University Press, 1989; English paperback edition, London: Faber and Faber, 1991), p. 111.

13 The reception of *Peeping Tom* is documented by Ian Christie in 'The Scandal of *Peeping Tom*', in Christie (ed.), *Powell, Pressburger and Others* (London: BFI, 1978), pp. 53–62.

14 V. F. Perkins, 'Charm and Blood', in *Oxford Opinion*, no. 42, October 1960, pp. 34–5; Wood, *Hitchcock's Films Revisited* (1965 section), p. 108.

15 Jonathan Coe, *James Stewart, Leading Man* (London: Bloomsbury, 1994), p. 153.

16 Susan White, '*Vertigo* and Problems of Knowledge in Feminist Film Theory', in Richard Allen and S. Ishii Gonzalès (eds), *Alfred Hitchcock: Centenary Essays* (London: BFI, 1999), p. 279.

17 Peter Conrad, *The Hitchcock Murders* (London: Faber and Faber, 1999), p. xi.

18 Sam Taylor, quoted in *Hitchcock* (BBC TV 1985, directed by Tristram Powell, for *Omnibus* series).

19 Hitchcock explained the 'icebox factor' in, for instance, an interview with Charles Thomas Samuels, in Samuels, *Encountering Directors* (New York: G. P. Putnams, 1972), p. 247.

20 Robert Carringer, *The Making of Citizen Kane* (London: John Murray, 1985), p. ix.

21 Hitchcock in the London *Evening News*, 16 November 1927, quoted in Donald Spoto, *The Life of Alfred Hitchcock: The Dark Side of Genius* (London: William Collins, 1983), p. 103. Contrast, in this respect, Michael Powell, who for all his single-mindedness was always more generous than Hitchcock in acknowledging collaborators; not only did he insist on the unique shared credit 'Written, produced and directed by Michael Powell and Emeric Pressburger', but even before that collaboration began he had ended his book on the filming of his very personal project, *The Edge of the World* (1938), with the reflection that 'in the long run it is good team-work that makes a good film'.

22 Carringer, *The Making of Citizen Kane*, p. x.

23 Royal Brown, 'Interview with Herrmann', in *High Fidelity*, September 1976, p. 65; quoted in Steven C. Smith, *A Heart at Fire's Center: The Life and Music of Bernard Herrmann* (Berkeley: University of California Press, 1991), p. 192.

24 Charles Barr, *English Hitchcock* (Moffat, Scotland: Cameron and Hollis, 1999); also 'Writing Screen Plays: Stannard and Hitchcock', in Andrew Higson (ed.), *Young and Innocent?: The Cinema in Britain 1896–1930* (Exeter University of Exeter Press, 2002).

25 Dan Auiler, *Vertigo: The Making of a Hitchcock Classic* (New York: St Martin's Press, 1998).

26 The first English translation, by Geoffrey Sainsbury, was entitled *The Living and the Dead* (London: Hutchinson, 1956); it was later reissued as *Vertigo* (London: Bloomsbury, 1997). Meanwhile, the French original had been reprinted in 1967 under the title given to the film in France, *Sueurs froides*. The film had gone into production under the title *From among the Dead*, a literal rendering of the novel's title.

27 *The Web of Lace* (from a novel), tx Sunday 21 September 1958; *Murder in Slow Motion* (from a play), tx Sunday 5 October 1958.

28 François Truffaut, *Hitchcock* (London: Secker & Warburg, 1968), p. 56. Originally published in French as *Le Cinéma selon Hitchcock* (Paris: Laffont, 1966).

29 This and other quotations about the preparation of *Vertigo* are taken, unless otherwise indicated, from the production files preserved in the Margaret Herrick Library of the Motion Picture Academy of Arts and Sciences, in Los Angeles.

30 Truffaut, *Hitchcock*, p. 57.

31 Spoto, *Life of Alfred Hitchcock*, p. 383. His account of the preparation of *Vertigo* is not free of other inaccuracies.

32 Auiler, *Vertigo*, pp. 44–8.

33 Bennett is interviewed in two screenwriter-based collections: Pat McGilligan (ed.), *Backstory* (Berkeley: University of California Press, 1986), and Lee Server (ed.), *Screenwriter Words Become Pictures* (Pittstown, NJ: Main Street Press, 1987).

34 Coe, *James Stewart*, p. 150.

35 Denis Norden, who collaborated with Coppel in England on two later scripts, told me that he never mentioned having worked with Hitchcock; possibly this was out of bitterness at the way his was treated after finishing work on *Vertigo* (phone conversation, May 1997).

36 Transcription of 'A Talk by Samuel Taylor', given at a conference at Pace University, New York, in June 1986, in Walter Raubicheck and Walter Srebnick (eds), *Hitchcock's Rereleased Films* (Detroit, MI: Wayne State University Press, 1991), p. 290.

37 The script of *Sabrina* is credited jointly to Ernest Lehman, who would write Hitchcock's next film after *Vertigo*, *North by Northwest*.

38 'A Talk by Samuel Taylor', pp. 288–9.

39 Taylor actually argued, at the 1986 conference, that the plot should have been revealed to the audience even earlier, by showing Elster and Judy together soon after Scottie's breakdown. 'A Talk by Samuel Taylor', pp. 290, 292.

40 Auiler, *Vertigo*, pp. 23–4.

41 James F. Maxfield, 'A Dreamer and his Dream: Another Way of Looking at Hitchcock's *Vertigo*', in *Film Criticism*, vol. 14 no. 3, Spring 1990, p. 3.

42 'One of Twins' was published in Bierce's collection *Can Such Things Be?* (1893); the other three stories referred to are from *In the Midst of Life: Stories of Soldiers and Civilians* (1892).

43 Hitchcock, interviewed in *Cinema* (US), vol. 1 no. 5, 1963, reprinted in Sid Gottlieb (ed.), *Hitchcock on Hitchcock* (London: Faber and Faber, 1995), p. 300.

44 Compare Cary Grant, older by a few months than Jessie Royce Landis, who played his mother in *North by Northwest*.

45 Robin Wood, *Hitchcock's Films Revisited*, pp. 380–3.

46 Maxfield, 'A Dreamer and his Dream', p. 5.

47 Coe, *James Stewart*, p. 157.

48 Truffaut, *Hitchcock*, p. 49.

49 Robert Corber uses this line in the title of his analysis of the film, ' "There are Many Such Stories": *Vertigo* and the Repression of Historical Knowledge', Chapter Five of Corber, *In the Name of National Security: Hitchcock, Homophobia and the Political Construction of Gender of in Postwar America* (Durham, NC: Duke University Press, 1993) – a good example of the extraordinary range of the literature on Hitchcock and *Vertigo* alluded to by Susan White (note 16 above).

50 Henry Bumstead, interviewed for BBC's 1986 *Omnibus* programme on Hitchcock (passage not used in final edit).

51 Wood, *Hitchcock's Films Revisited*, pp. 380–2.

52 Auiler records the amount of reshooting that was needed to get this long and intricate scene right, causing the film to go over schedule and budget, *Vertigo*, p. 118. For a sensitive

account of the contribution of the actors in this
scene and elsewhere, see Doug Tomlinson,
'"They Should be Treated Like Cattle":
Hitchcock and the Question of Performance',
in *Hitchcock's Rereleased Films*, pp. 95ff.
53 Auiler, *Vertigo*, pp. 161–2.
54 'A Talk by Samuel Taylor', p. 297. The
epilogue scene is included in the laserdisc
edition of *Vertigo*.
55 Maxfield, 'A Dreamer and his Dream',
p. 3ff.

56 Wood, *Hitchcock's Films Revisited* (1965
section), p. 120.
57 Ibid. p. 117.
58 Ibid. (1989 section), p. 385.
59 Chris Marker, 'A Free Replay (notes on
Vertigo)', in John Boorman and Walter
Donohue (eds), *Projections 4½* (London: Faber
and Faber, 1995), p. 124. First published in
French in *Positif* magazine.
60 'A Talk by Samuel Taylor', p. 297.

CREDITS

· ·

Vertigo

USA
1958

Directed by
Alfred Hitchcock
Screenplay by
Alec Coppel, Samuel Taylor
Based upon the novel
D'entre les morts by Pierre
Boileau, Thomas Narcejac
Director of Photography
Robert Burks
Edited by
George Tomasini
Art Direction
Hal Pereira, Henry
Bumstead
Music by
Bernard Herrmann

©Alfred J. Hitchcock
Productions Inc

Production Company
a Paramount release
Associate Producer
Herbert Coleman
[Production Manager
C.O. 'Doc' Erickson]
[2nd Unit Directors
Herbert Coleman, John P.
Fulton]
Assistant Director
Daniel McCauley
[Script Supervisor
Peggy Robertson]
**[Second Unit
Photography**
William Williams, Irmin
Roberts, Loyal Griggs]
[Camera Operators
Leonard South
2nd Unit:
Buddy Weiler, Kyme Meade,
Fred Kaiffer]
Special Sequence by
John Ferren
**Special Photographic
Effects**
John P. Fulton
Process Photography
Farciot Edouart, Wallace
Kelley
**Technicolor Colour
Consultant**
Richard Mueller
Set Decoration
Sam Comer, Frank McKelvy
Costumes
Edith Head
Make-up Supervision
Wally Westmore
Hairstyle Supervision
Nellie Manley
Titles Designed by
Saul Bass
[Optical Effects
Paul K. Lerpae]
Music Conducted by
Muir Mathieson

Sound Recording by
Harold Lewis, Winston
Leverett
[Stunt Double
Polly Burson]
[Stand-in for Kim Novak
Jean Corbett]

Cast
James Stewart
John 'Scottie' Ferguson
Kim Novak
Judy Barton/'Madeleine
Elster'
Barbara Bel Geddes
Midge
Tom Helmore
Gavin Elster
Henry Jones
the coroner
Raymond Bailey
doctor
Ellen Corby
McKittrick Hotel
manageress
Konstantin Shayne
Pop Leibel
Lee Patrick
new owner of Madeleine's
car

[uncredited]
Fred Graham
falling policeman
Alfred Hitchcock
man walking past shipyard
office
Buck Harrington
gateman
Bess Flowers
Forbes Murray
customers at Ernie's
Rolando Gotti
maître d' at Ernie's
Bruno Della Santina
waiter at Ernie's

Carlo Dotto
bartender at Ernie's
Joanne Genthon
Carlotta Valdes in portrait
Paul Bryar
Detective Captain Hansen
William Remick
jury foreman
Ed Stevlingson
attorney
Dori Simmons
mistaken identity in
restaurant
Jack Richardson
male escort
Nina Shipman
mistaken identity in art
gallery
Julian Petruzzi
flower seller
Margaret Brayton
Miliza Milo
saleswomen
Roxann Delmar
model

Don Giovanni
John Benson
salesmen
Molly Dodd
beauty operator
Sara Taft
nun in tower
June Jocelyn
Miss Woods
Jack Ano
extra

11,511 feet
128 minutes

Colour by
Technicolor
VistaVision
MPAA: 18867

Credits compiled by
Markku Salmi,
BFI Filmographic Unit

ALSO PUBLISHED

If you would like further information about future BFI Film Classics or about other books on film, media and popular culture from BFI Publishing, please write to:

BFI Film Classics
BFI Publishing
21 Stephen Street
London W1P 2LN